GESTALTING ADDICTION

Speaking Truth to Addiction:
Its Power, Definition,
Theory, Therapy, and Treatment

Dr. Angela Brownemiller

Publication #20
Dr. Angela® Theory and Practice Collection
Metaterra® Publications

GESTALTING ADDICTION

Speaking Truth to Addiction:
Its Power, Definition,
Theory, Therapy, and Treatment

Publication #20
Dr. Angela® Theory and Practice Collection

Dr. Angela Brownemiller

Illustrated by Angela Brownemiller
Metaterra® Publications

Metaterra® Publications

GESTALTING ADDICTION:

Speaking Truth to Addiction: Its Power, Definition, Theory, Therapy, and Treatment
Publication #20: Dr. Angela® Theory and Practice Collection

Copyright © 2020, and 2000, 2005, 2010, 2013, 2014, 2015, 2016, 2017, 2018, 2019
Angela Brownemiller / Angela Browne-Miller.
Copyright © 2020, and 2000, 2005, 2010, 2013, 2014, 2015, 2016, 2017, 2018, 2019
Metaterra® Publications.

Published in the United States by Metaterra® Publications.
HYPERLINK "http://www.Metaterra.com"
www.Metaterra.com   www.Amazon.com
Library of Congress Cataloging-in-Publication Data.
Brownemiller, Angela.
GESTALTING ADDICTION
Angela Brownemiller / Angela Browne-Miller
1. Consciousness. 2. Psychology. 3. Biology.
4. Addiction. 5. Chemical Dependence. 6. Gestalt.
7. Twelve Step. 8. Therapy. 9. Gregory Bateson.
10. Angela Brownemiller. 11. Angela Browne-Miller.
ISBN 13: 978-1-937951283 (Paperback).
Also see Amazon for Ebook.
Published in the United States of America for US and worldwide distribution.
Metaterra® Publications, Metaterra.com (See this url for postal address).
GESTALTING ADDICTION by and copyright © Angela Brownemiller.
Cover and content illustrations, charts, diagrams, text,
by and copyright ©Angela Brownemiller.
Book and cover design by and copyright ©Angela Brownemiller.
HYPERLINK "Info@Metaterra.com"
Metaterra.com   DrAngela.com   KeysToSelf.com

GESTALTING ADDICTION is based upon the material presented in *SEEING THE HIDDEN FACE OF ADDICTION: DETECTING AND CONFRONTING THIS INVASIVE PRESENCE* which is written for lay persons and their counselors, psychotherapists, clinicians, and guides.

SEEING THE HIDDEN FACE OF ADDICTION

Detecting and Confronting This Invasive Presence

Dr. Angela Brownemiller

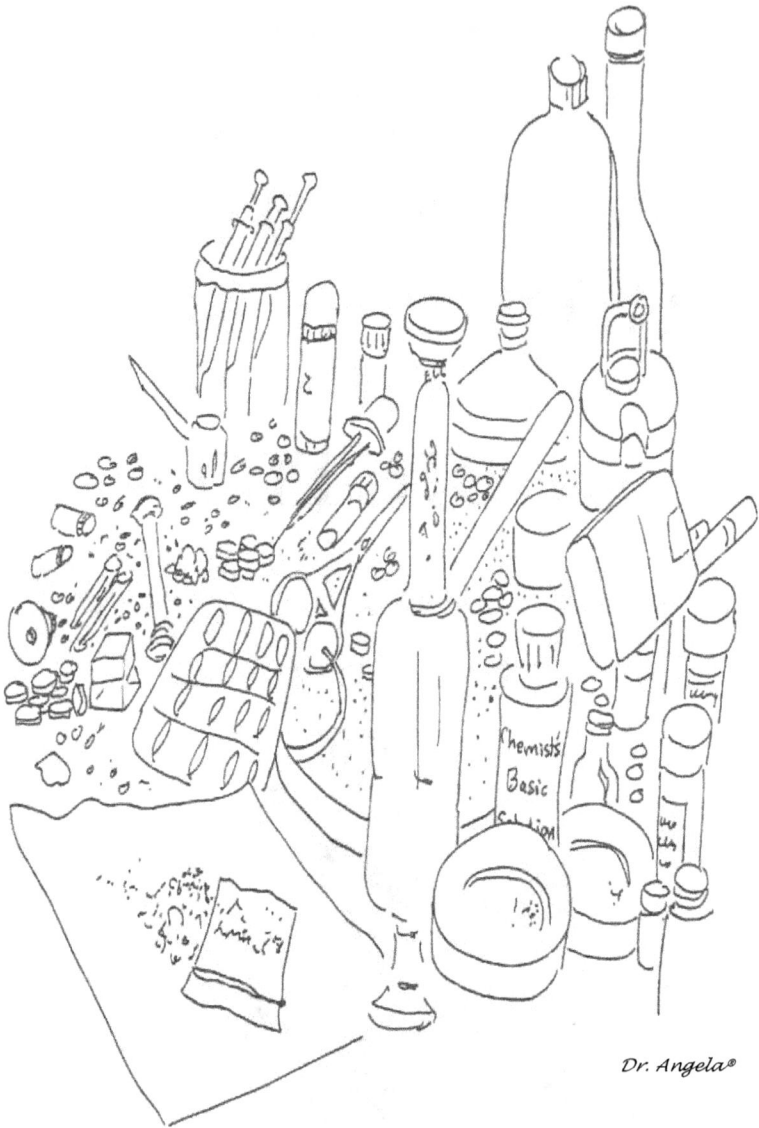

Truth About Addiction

Table of Contents

Gestalting Definitions   **11**
Gestalting (verb)   11
Gestalt (noun)   13
Gestalt Theory   13
Gestalt Psychology   13
Gestalt Learning and the Double Bind   15
Gestalten   17
Gestalt and The AHA   19
Gestalt Therapy   21
Gestalt Therapy, continued   23

Part One:
About This Book   **25**
1. Note to Readers   27
2. Introduction to Gestalting Addiction:
    Overview of This Book   29
3. Some Background   51

Part Two:
Toward Gestalting Addiction   **65**
4. The Gestalt AHA   67
5. Toward Higher Levels of Knowing: Gestalt Learning   87
6. Clarifying, Revising, and Reviving Gestalt on a
    New Platform: Gestalting Addiction Itself   105

Part Three:
Faces of Gestalt   **111**
7. Toward Unveiling the True Gestalt   113
8. Faces of Gestalt   123

Part Four:
Looking Beyond Known Addiction
    For the Actual Addiction   **141**
9. Denial & Confrontation of Denial: Recipe for What?   143
10. Seeing Past Addiction and Addiction
    Treatment Paradigms   153

11. Cautionary Note on Medically Assisted Treatment
        and Psychedelically Assisted Treatment   157
12. Confronting Addiction: Addiction, Reveal Yourself   163

Part Five:
Unveiling Addiction for What the Addiction Is   **169**
13. Addiction Inhabits   171
14. Gestalting the Trojan Horse Camouflaging
        The Truth About Addiction   177
15. The Identified Addict   181
16. On Deleting This Thing We Call Addiction   187

Part Six:
Unveiling, Gestalting, and Confronting
        The Addiction in Therapy   **195**
17. About Part Six: On Gestalting the
        Paradox of Addiction   197
18. Seeing the Power of Paradox   203
19. Seeing the Four Basic (and Repeatable) Stages
        Of Our Journey   213
20. Mapping the Four Basic Stages/Patterns
        of Our Journey   227
21. Recognizing and Facing Ingrained
        Problem Pattern Addiction   235
22. Undrugging the Feelings   245
23. The Going Conscious Process   253
24. Gestalting the Addiction   261
25. Addiction Gestalting Itself   269
26. Navigating the Emotional Terrain
        In Gestalting Addiction   283

Epilog: The Truth About Us   **295**
Booklist and Recommended Reading   303, 304
About the Author   305

Illustrations, Diagrams, Charts

Truth About Addiction	6
AHA	10
"I see you addiction, here in the chair."	25
"Can this be me?"	65
Is This an Infected AHA?	84
Two of the Brain's Numerous Problem Solving Scenarios	86
Problem/Challenge: To Leave the Problem Pattern (Cycle)	103
Problem/Challenge: Differentiating the Self from Problem Pattern	109
Face to Face	111
Law of Closure: The Form Completion Gestalt	125
A → B	129
Confine Us to This Picture: Spill Us Back Into The Cycle	129
Attentive Processing	137
"I'm looking for the *Light*."	141
What Addiction Appears to Be → What Addiction Actually Is	165
"Addiction, I see past your mask."	169
"Addiction, I see you now. Think you can fool me?"	195
Programming of Organism vs. Programming of Addiction	199
Paradox	203
New Level of Understanding and Awareness	203
Paradox Paradox Paradox	208
AHA! Release	210
Struggle	217, 218
Paradox Chart	219
A → B: Trigger Urge Craving Addictive Response Cycle	220
Insight	221, 222
Elevation	223, 224
Journey of Four Stages/Patterns	225
Mapping Our Stages	230-234
Reality Form Completion	248
Infected Form Completion into Addiction Pattern	248
Let My Addiction Go	263
Chair to Chair	272
Communication with the Addiction	273
Cycle to Cycle	275
Addiction in Both Chairs	276
SUMMARIZING DIAGRAM: True Problem Challenge	289
Facings	290,291
Anonymous	299
In the Circle of Self	301
What is Unspoken	307

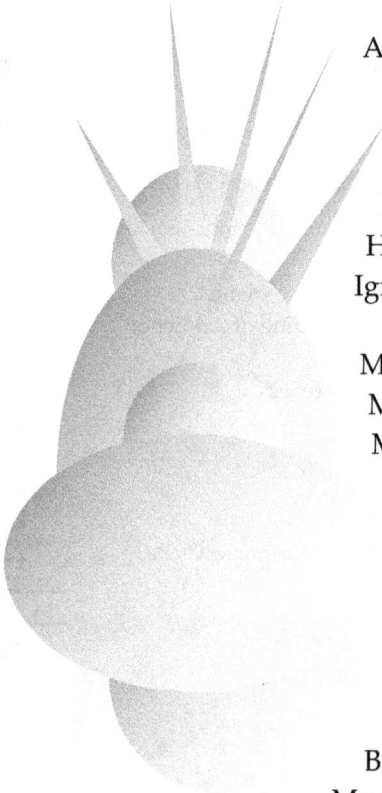

AHA!

Precious
moment
Prescient wave
Heart spark
Igniting possibility.

Moment pacing time
Mirroring hope
Manifesting soul
Salvaging self
Reaching out
(and in).

Longing so dear
So close to center
Where we store fragments
Bits of the whole we are...
More so
Bits of who we can be.

AHA!

GESTALTING DEFINITIONS

This book includes this author's current views on ADDICTION and on GESTALT[1] (and on the "NEW GESTALT") as per various gestalt principles, interpretations, (also perhaps misinterpretations), areas of scientific investigation, psychological applications, forms of psychotherapy, as well as applicabilities to addiction treatment—including significant extensions of the concepts of gestalt and of addiction itself. The implications of the notion of gestalt are profound and can move into new domains of realization and practice. Some of the terms and ideas that are relevant to this discussion of both **gestalt** *and* **addiction,** *and of what this author is herein defining as* **gestalting addiction,** *include the following....*

Gestalting (verb):

Defined by this author, Dr. Angela Brownemiller, as being a verb derived from the noun, GESTALT. In essence, the GESTALTING described herein is the *act or process* of the perceiving or deriving (or detecting or revealing) of a whole or more whole picture (or greater understanding or "truth") by allowing (or perceiving) parts to suggest the whole they are components of – while also suggesting a whole that is actually more than the sum of its parts or apparent parts. This verb, *gestalting,* also suggests an unveiling or AHA process -- a form completion, closure, realization.

The mind/brain's parallel **gestalting process** can be exemplified by the mind/brain's closing a broken circle, **seeing, gestalting, the whole** rather than a part of the whole as pictured here:

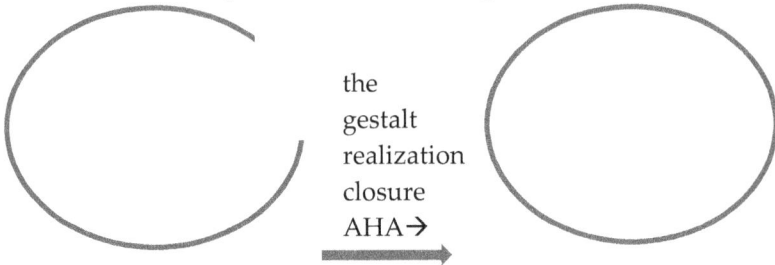

the
gestalt
realization
closure
AHA→

---

[1] Origin 1920: the German word, *gestalt,* pronounced *guh-shtalt,* refers to: form, shape; an organized field, pattern, or configuration that cannot be derived from the sum of its parts; a unified whole. Plural: *gestalts, gestalten.* Derived from the German philosophy of *gestaltqualitat,* meaning form or shape, exploring the notion of perception.

gestalt (noun) *plural* gestalts *also* gestalten:

"Something such as a structure or experience that, when considered as a whole, has qualities that are **more than the total of all its parts**." *Cambridge English Dictionary*

"*Broadly:* The general quality or character of something." *Merriam-Webster Dictionary*

"The word GESTALT is used in modern German to mean the way a thing has been 'placed,' or 'put together.' There is no exact equivalent in English. 'Form' and 'shape' are the usual translations; in psychology the word is often interpreted as 'pattern' or 'configuration'." *Encyclopedia Britannica*

gestalt theory:

"[This] influential [early 20th century] theory of perception... proposed that perception was determined not by the elemental sensations of light and dark but by laws of similarity, good continuation (analogous to smoothness), closure, symmetry, etc. that grouped such elements within a **larger** visual **context**. The founder of this school, Max Wertheimer [described] 'phi motion,' the illusory percept of smooth motion that appears when a spot of light flashes in sequence over a set of discrete points in space; this illusion of motion – which underlies our perception of smooth motion in movies – **cannot be reduced** to its underlying elemental light flashes." *Encyclopedia of Neuroscience*

gestalt psychology:

"A school of psychology founded in the 20th century that provided the foundation for the modern study of perception. [Related] gestalt theory emphasizes that ... the **attributes of the whole are not deducible from analysis of the parts in isolation**." *Encyclopedia Britannica*

gestalt learning and the double bind:

"The concepts of **deutero-learning** and **double bind** have acquired an increasingly important status in various fields of social and behavioral science. [These are] defined very briefly as, respectively, **learning to learn** and **pathological deutero-learning**....[Gregory Bateson[2] defined] **simple learning** [as] **'proto-learning'** [aka: single loop learning], the adaptation of behavior in response to contingencies of reinforcement. **Gestalt learning** [aka: learning to learn] **was defined as 'deutero-learning,'** the changes in proto-learning as a result of **'insight'** into the structure (or class) of the situation in which proto-learning takes place."

Max Visser, *Gregory Bateson on Deutero-Learning and Double Bind*

"... {The] organizational structure of A.A. [Alcoholics Anonymous] presented points of great interest to systems theory.... My debt to A.A. will be evident throughout—also...my respect for its co-founders, Bill W. and Dr. Bob. ... [Also note] the famous *Serenity Prayer:*[3] 'God grant us the serenity to accept the things we cannot change, courage to change the things we can, and wisdom to know the difference.' If double binds cause anguish and despair ... then it follows, conversely, that for healing these wounds ... some converse of [release from] the double bind will be appropriate. The double bind leads to ... despair [saying], 'There are no alternatives.' The *Serenity Prayer* explicitly frees the worshipper from these maddening bonds."

Gregory Bateson, *The Cybernetics of "Self:" A Theory of Alcoholism*

---

[2] I am forever grateful to Gregory Bateson for the impact he has had on my thinking, world view, and life. I was fortunate to be accepted at age 19 (as one of two undergraduates in a room full of graduate students and professors) into two years of bi weekly seminars with Gregory Bateson. I know so many thinkers, professionals, and others who have carried Bateson's concepts into their own fields and work. I have found Bateson's *notions of gestalt learning (deutero-learning)* and the *acquisition of insight* to be particularly relevant in my work with people—and with the human mind, human emotions and cognitions, and human behaviors.

[3] The *Serenity Prayer* was written by American theologian Reinhold Neibuhr in approximately 1930. The prayer became widely known when A.A. began using it in 1941.

gestalten:

"To organize, arrange, structure, shape, carry out, fashion, mold, give artistic or literary form; to become, develop or turn into something."

Shorter Oxford English Dictionary, 2002
Harper Collins German Dictionary, 2004

"You will learn the integrated communication methods as you complete the next step in your mental education. This is a **gestalten** function which will overlay data paths in your awareness, resolving complexities and masses of input from the mentat index-catalogue techniques which you already have mastered. Your initial problem will be the breaking tensions arising from the divergent assembly of mentat overlay integration, you can be immersed in the Babel Problem, which is the label we give to the **omnipresent dangers of achieving wrong combinations from accurate information**."

Frank Herbert,
Excerpt from the fictional "Mentat Handbook"
in *The Children of Dune* (of the *Dune Series*)

"Bateson said, '…The individual nexus of pathways which I call 'me' is no longer so precious because the nexus is only part of the larger mind….' What then would an ecological ethic of relating [to oneself and others] look like? It must be, at once, an ethic that favors the larger *gestalten* in the systemic world, promotes an extended sense of self among humans, and also helps us to live in a fully sustainable interaction within the biosphere…."

Noel G. Charlton,
Understanding Gregory Bateson: Mind, Beauty, and the Sacred Truth

"The 'self' is a false reification of an improperly delimited part of this much larger field of interlocking processes."

Gregory Bateson,
Steps to an Ecology of Mind

gestalt and the AHA:

"No problem can be solved from the same level of consciousness that created it."   Albert Einstein

"An 'aha' experience is quite simply a moment of sudden insight. Often it will be preceded by a period of stuckness, an impasse, and surface as the client begins to accept that impasse or make an authentic movement away from it. The client reconfigures [her or his] field. When this reorganization occurs, a new integration of the situation falls into place as the client creatively adjusts to [his or her] field differently. Much excitement is generated as the 'aha' experience forms; everything seems to make sense in the moment of 'coming together.' ... At such times the therapist's unobtrusive presence can lead seemingly magically to the client **integrating in one swift moment** what has been experienced to date as disparate parts or fragments. This is the 'aha' experience."
                          Dave Mann, *Gestalt Therapy: 100 Key Points and Techniques*

"You know the sweet satisfaction when you suddenly have an epiphany? I'm talking about that 'Aha!' moment when the **circuits suddenly connect** and, seemingly out of nowhere, you are **struck with an insight**. ... Today, using fMRI technology, neuroscientists can watch the revelation unfold on a cellular level. Neurons begin to cluster and activity speeds up, eventually giving way to bursts of energy not unlike a mini fireworks show. All this can be witnessed by the fMRI technician about eight seconds before the subject is aware of [her or his] impending moment of truth."   Robert Best, *The Science of Epiphany*, BestMindFrame.com

"There are two general cognitive strategies which people use to solve problems. SEARCH involves systematic evaluation of possible problem states intervening between the current state and the goal state, and the use of available operators to transform one state into another. ... Another general strategy for problem solving involves INSIGHT .... Insight is the **sudden awareness of the solution to a problem** (i.e., the "Aha!" phenomenon) with little or no conscious access to the processing leading up to that solution.... The notion of sudden insight ... has been identified as an important characteristic of creative thought...."
          John Hounis, et. al., *The Origins of Insight in Resting-State Brain Activity*,
                                                  Neuropsychologia. 2008:1/15:46(1)

gestalt therapy:

"Gestalt therapy is a client-centered approach to psychotherapy that helps clients focus on the present and understand what is really happening in their lives right now, rather than what they may perceive to be happening based on past experience. Instead of simply talking about past situations, clients are encouraged to experience them, perhaps through re-enactment. Through the gestalt process, clients learn to become more aware of how their own negative thought patterns and behaviors are blocking true self-awareness....

"Gestalt therapy emphasizes that to alleviate unresolved anger, pain, anxiety, resentment, and other negative feelings, these emotions cannot just be discussed, but **must be actively expressed in the present time.** If that doesn't happen, both **psychological and physical symptoms can arise."**   Psychology Today, *psychologytoday.com*

"Thus the therapeutic core of gestalt therapy is **increasing awareness**."
Eleanor O'Leary, *Gestalt Therapy Around the World*

"The **empty chair technique** is a quintessential gestalt therapy exercise that places the person in therapy across from an empty chair. He or she is asked to imagine that someone (such as a boss, spouse, or relative) [...] or a part of themselves is sitting in the chair. **The therapist encourages dialogue between the empty chair and person in therapy.... Sometimes the roles are reversed and the person in therapy assumes the metaphorical person or part of a person in the chair. The empty chair technique can be especially useful for helping people become mindful of the whole situation and forgotten or disengaged pieces of their own [selves]....**

"Another common exercise in gestalt therapy is the exaggeration exercise. During this exercise, the person in therapy is asked to repeat and exaggerate a particular movement or expression, such as frowning or bouncing a leg, in order to make the person **more aware of the emotions attached to the behavior.**"
Good Therapy, *goodtherapy.org*

gestalt therapy, continued:

"Gestalt therapy brings phenomenology into the clinical setting[:] what a client is (and is not) *aware* of, what stands out as *figure,* and how the client *understands* and ascribes *meaning* to the experience."
Stephanie Sabar, What's a Gestalt? Gestalt Review. 2013:17(1)

"The founders of gestalt therapy, Fritz and Laura Perls, had worked with Kurt Goldstein, a neurologist who had applied principles of gestalt psychology to the functioning of the organism."
Bernd Bocian, Fritz Perls in Berlin 1893-
1933

"The extent to which gestalt psychology influenced gestalt therapy is disputed, however. In any case it [gestalt therapy] is not identical with gestalt psychology."
Joe Wysong/Edward Rosenfeld, An Oral History of Gestalt
Therapy

"What Fritz Perls has done has been to take a few terms from gestalt psychology, stretch their meaning beyond recognition, mix them with notions—often unclear and often incompatible—from the depth psychologies, existentialism, and common sense, and he has called the whole mixture gestalt therapy. His work has no substantive relation to scientific gestalt psychology. To use his own language, Fritz Perls has done 'his thing'; whatever it is, it is *not* gestalt psychology."
Mary Henle, Gestalt Psychology and Gestalt Therapy,
Pres. Address to Div. 24 APA Mtg, 1975

"The development of gestalt therapy has been associated in the popular mind with the aggressive, dramatic, and unusual personality of the late Fritz Perls. But now it is coming to general awareness within the field of psychotherapy that much of what was considered gestalt therapy is but one particular form and that **Laura Perls made equally substantial contributions**." Ava Serlin and Paul Shane,
Laura Perls and Gestalt Therapy: Her Life and Values

Part One:

About This Book

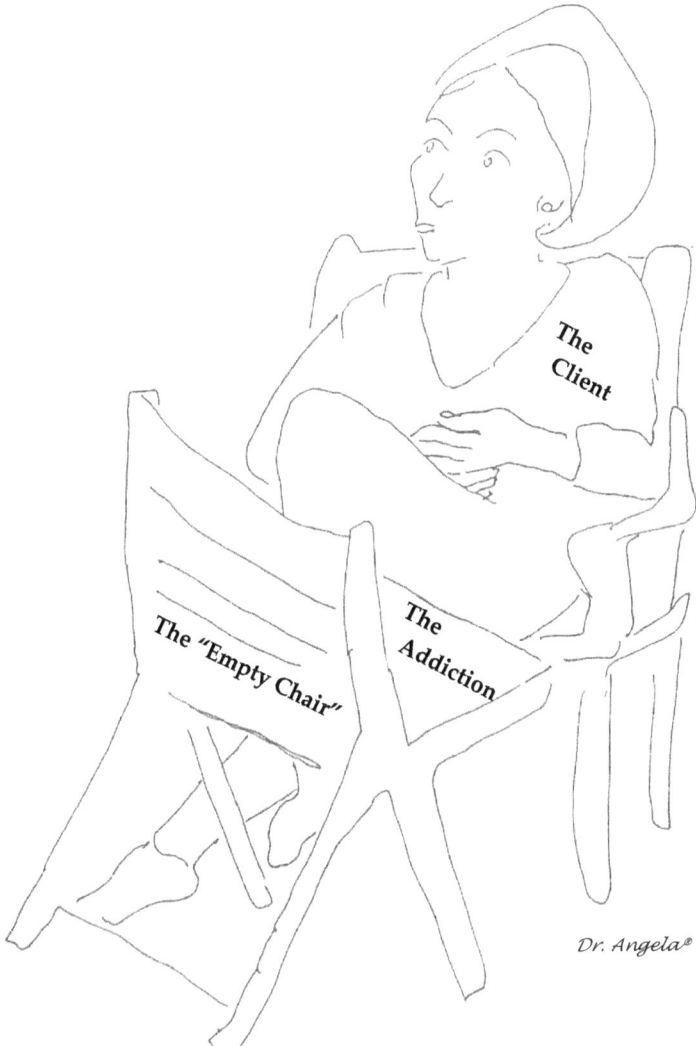

The Client

The "Empty Chair"

The Addiction

Dr. Angela®

"I see you, addiction, here in the chair."

1
Note to Readers

I offer this brief discussion to lay persons, concerned people in all walks of life, including but not limited to clients and patients in (or considering) therapy and or treatment for drug and alcohol, and or nondrug (other behavioral and emotional) states of mind, habit, and addiction. This includes most every one of us in some way as we are all creatures of habit and/or what I call "co-habit," creatures of co-habit.

You, we, have a right to know questions and issues in "the field," matters affecting your, our, choices in life, as well as in therapy and or treatment.

I also offer this discussion to those clinicians, practitioners, advocates, advisors, enforcers, and adjudicators (including social workers, psychologists, counselors, nurses, psychiatrists, physicians, faith leaders, law enforcement officers, attorneys, judges, policy makers, and so many others) who are addressing human issues and struggles. We best understand what is actually going on, what kind of power and control factors we are actually facing.

Power? Yes, power. It is time to speak truth to power, not only to the power of addiction treatment models and paradigms, and not only to those who seek to control definitions of treatment and of addiction, even of diagnosis, but to speak truth to addiction itself. Addiction is far more than we have yet seen (acknowledged) it as being. Addiction is ubiquitous, within our nature, intrinsic to our neural wiring. Yet, we are <u>not</u> our addictions.

2
Introduction to
Gestalting Addiction:
Overview of this Book

This book, *GESTALTING ADDICTION*, is a conversation with Readers. This book is also a conversation with the human mind and a powerful element registering within the human mind: **addiction**.

This book is ultimately a conversation with addiction itself, seeking to pull down the disguise, to reveal addiction for what it is—to gestalt addiction itself, or better stated to invite addiction to gestalt itself. You see, the truth is out there, or best to restate this, the truth is in here, deep within our minds/brains, and our SELVES.[4]

In the flow of this conversation on the following pages is addiction to substances, and to behaviors whether or not these involve drugs/substances. Included in the addictions I refer to herein are not only behavioral patterns, cycles, habits, but also emotional and even cognitive patterns, cycles, habits (as well as patterns of perception).

----

[4] See recommended reading listed at the end of this book. I delve more deeply into the functions of the mind/brain and their effect upon our realizing who and what we are in other of my books, such as *OVERRIDING THE EXTINCTION SCENARIO (Part One): DETECTING THE BAR ON THE EVOLUTION OF THE HUMAN SPECIES*. Also see the in depth look at addiction in the series which I edited, the *INTERNATIONAL COLLECTION ON ADDICTIONS*.

As I explain in *Part Five* of this book, I have come to see problem addiction as an **opportunistic matrix**, an **invasive patterning working its way so very deeply into our brain's networks that it can invade and even subsume our basic and even executive mental functions (such as thought organization, decision making, and moral judgement).** More than this, addiction can be so invasive it can even consume pieces of our own identity, causing us to almost feel that we are the addiction itself.

**At some point
the boundaries
between ourselves
and our addiction programming
can be compromised, confused.**

LET'S NOT FOOL OURSELVES

We are all addicts. We all carry addiction programming. We are lifeforms that function according to deep programming, even according to programmed-in addiction to our deep programming.[5] Yes, environment plays a central role in all we do and are. However, we also are wired, genetically, to develop the biological wiring that programs us to live and adapt within our environments.

Much of this programming has definite survival and functional value. I therefore use the term, *problem addiction,* to differentiate between healthy addiction programming and unhealthy *problem* addiction programming (which is programming to develop and

---

[5] I share a more creative and philosophical discussion of this programming in UNVEILING THE HIDDEN INSTINCT. See reading list at the end of this present book, GESTALTING ADDICTION, for more information.

maintain unhealthy *problem* patterns). In essence, our deepest programming to become so very addicted is running awry in far too many instances. Hence we see too many of us falling prey to drug/alcohol, behavioral, emotional, and other very troubled and dangerous patternings, cycles, addictions.

WE HAVE SEEN THE ADDICT
AND HE/SHE/IT IS
<u>NOT</u> US

Let me emphasize this right here, out the gate: We may *appear to be* the problem pattern addict, not because we are addicted, rather because the problem addiction programming has infiltrated, even overtaken, pieces of us: invaded, subsumed, us: become more and more of who we are (or feel we are).

I have found this notion of invasion, of infiltrating right down into the identity, to be highly relevant in working with persons who are experiencing problem addictions. I have seen that we are treating, speaking to, the person, yes, but also to the invading programming. Calling this invader out, gestalting this addiction program, brings us face to face with the programming holding us hostage. (See especially *Parts Five* and *Six* of this book.)

ON GESTALT

In the process of this conversation with Readers, with the human mind, and with addiction itself, I refer to elements of gestalt theory and practice, such as the principles of perception forming the gestalt theory that defined itself early in the 20th century, and ensuing application of these principles. I also address one of the basic critiques of these principles, which centers on the matter of these principles referring to what they suggested were basically "innate" brain tendencies or functions affecting the way we see.

Clearly, all these years later, we now know and can demonstrate scientifically much more about the impact of environment (and of experience within that environment) on perception, and on thought, emotion, behavior, on the mind/brain itself. Few if any aspects of our biological (including brain) processes occur independently of the effects of environment.

To isolate from environment the functions of the biological brain, to develop principles of perception of that environment based only on what appears to be our brain's inherited programming and wiring, now makes little sense.

Ultimately, principles of perception, of how we see/feel/perceive our environments and experiences, must reflect the effect of environment and of experience within environment on perception itself. Not only is our response to perception environmentally contingent, even environmentally impacted, our perception itself is.

So where there are certainly deeply ingrained neural and even synaptic brain mechanisms and programs forming perception processes, rarely if ever do these function unaffected by (or in the absence of) environmental influences.

ADDICTION DRIVEN PERCEPTION

This understanding is clearly relevant when talking about addiction, as addiction is a brain process/function, yes. Yet addiction is a brain program (process/function) that interacts with environment (and with perceptions of environment) to activate, even to endure. (We see this quite clearly in substance addiction as many perceived "triggers" appear to us to be "found" in the environment.)

Addiction pattern programming affects, interferes in, even invades, brain functions including perception and attention to perception. Hence, what I describe as *addiction driven perception* must be recognized and addressed in working with persons affected by problem addiction programming. Let's start by looking at perception, addiction, and environment….

DERIVATIVE IDEAS
RELEVANT TO ADDICTION

While early 20th century principles speaking of perception's "innate" gestalt functions have been researched, tested, expanded upon, critiqued, counter proposed, there are elements that nevertheless remain valuable, most specifically a central notion of gestalt, which is that **the whole is greater than the sum of its parts**. Here, I add a few logical derivatives to this key principle, which are that:

(a) The whole or what we perceive (of the whole) is derived via some aspect of a **gestalt or form completion process**, as pictured in the first diagram on the first page of the definitions at the opening of this book. I define this "form" completion as GESTALT<u>ING</u>.

(b) The brain's form completion function is key in particular survival-like situations. For example, in "the wild," detecting a predator coming toward us may require our brain to rapidly knit together and expand upon whatever fragmented data we have (such as sounds, shadows, images, etc.) to complete the picture of the approaching danger, so that we can best respond to this unseen or not fully seen danger.

(c) The whole that we perceive is NOT NECESSARILY ENTIRELY ACCURATE, rather is the product of the brain's gestalt function, its **form completion** or what I also describe as its **reality estimation** process.

(c) What we see is not all there is to see: it REMAINS A PARTIAL PICTURE. While what we believe we do see is not necessarily accurate, it is also not necessarily complete, rather is the **reality estimation** I refer to above.

(d) The word "see" here can be extended to *perceive, sense, feel, believe, and so on*. I therefore say that the form completion or *reality estimation* process I refer to above is present in visual as well as in OTHER PERCEPTUAL (AND RESULTING EMOTIONAL AND BEHAVIORAL) PROCESSES.

(e) When realized as a **LEAP** in perception, in knowing, the experience of *suddenly gestalting* the greater picture indeed has a seeming suddenness to it, an AHA. This AHA is powerful and still to be fully and effectively understood and applied in treatment and therapy.

(g) **THE WHOLE PICTURE, YES, EVEN THE WHOLE FEELING, EMOTION, EXPERIENCE, ETC. IS GREATER THAN THE SUM OF ITS PARTS.**

Also note:

(h) Just as what is really going on around us is a partial picture, what we feel is really going on inside us is also a partial picture.

(i) Even what we believe we are feeling and experiencing is just the tip of the iceberg. There is much more to what we are experiencing and feeling than we know there to be. **Addiction treatment and therapy must take this matter into account. For example, a craving or *relapse pull* sensation is a partial picture of what is going on inside us.**

(j) When we experience the whole we are not necessarily putting the parts together to induce (and deduce) the whole with accuracy. What results is not necessarily an accurate picture of the whole, if one is at all possible given the brain functions that gestalt (form complete) this picture.[6]

Each of the above points is central in understanding that a problem addiction program can force what I tell my clients is an *infected gestalt*. This *infected gestalt* incorrectly completes a picture or pattern, even an impulse, to pressure its host—US—to respond to a trigger via what I call the:

impulse to relapse
or the
relapse reflex.

WHEN OUR BRAIN COMPLETES THE PICTURE, AT LEAST "A" PICTURE

Our brains complete pictures or perceptions (of objects, experiences, emotions, sensations, so-called "triggers," etc.) we may want to or need to see (know, sense) when we cannot see all there is about the whole. I extend this model beyond the basic visual to other forms of perception, even to what I describe herein as **emotional perception, emotion driven perception**, and **addiction driven perception**.

---

[6] I suggest that: Perhaps we are *wired not to know* the whole, *programmed with inherent limitations in knowing*. See this book for more on this notion: *UNVEILING THE HIDDEN INSTINCT*, as per reading list at the end of this present book, *GESTALTING ADDICTION*.

I note that the accuracy of conclusions (about the "whole") that our brain draws, "knowings" regarding "what is really going on," are always by nature based on partial information (as we can never see and know all there is to see/know). Our brain's conclusions about our reality are generally taken for granted, taken to be reality, yet of course are to be questioned.[7]

How often do we see persons coming to conclusions about what is going on that may or may not relate to what is actually going on?

How frequently is the substance addicted person pulled back into relapse, back into a use cycle, by cravings that appear to be saying relapse will be release from longing, withdrawal, and or other suffering? What forms of incorrect picture (including cravings) do our addictions present us with in order for us to fall back into their addiction patterns and cycles?

**Is this perhaps
the fly in the ointment, the...**

flaw in the gestalt:
**the possibility that
form completion can
distort reality rather than simply fill in gaps.**

---

[7] This is also a question to be asked when working in the area of psychotherapy where gestalt-like techniques are being applied (wittingly or unwittingly), and or where conducting gestalt therapy itself. Is what we think we are seeing, sensing, feeling what we are actually seeing, sensing, feeling? How do we proceed when we do not know? Can gestaltING allow us to see, sense, feel more of what is really going on inside our minds/brains?

This flaw in the gestalt allows (or even directs) incorrect information and related assumptions to fill in gaps, to erroneously or dangerously form/complete a picture, even to form/complete/*trigger* an unhealthy pattern. This gestalt or form completion process can be powerfully affected by the impact on the brain of the addiction itself.[8])

INDUCING INCORRECT CONCLUSIONS

So we can think/feel/see an incorrect larger picture, induce a perhaps incorrect conclusion, as if this is being correctly perceived, witnessed, gestalted, by our minds/brains. Our brains, our minds, our emotional perceptions, can draw, in a powerful wave, an *overarching conclusory gestalt,* complete an incomplete or even incorrect conclusion/pattern, forming a *flawed gestalt AHA.*

Note: It appears that problem addictions and their patterns are designed to generate flawed gestalts that respond to, and even generate, cravings, even sense opportunities for cravings, with a pull of the addiction pattern's host—of us —into the trigger-urge then response-by-relapse/using pattern.

The problem pattern stays alive by keeping us trapped in it.

---

[8] I develop this further in other publications. See: opening chapters of *TRANSCENDING ADDICTION, 2ND Edition;* psychobiological material in the *INTERNATIONAL COLLECTION ON ADDICTIONS;* also discussion of neuroscientific information and the brain in *OVERRIDING THE EXTINCTION SCENARIO, Part One.* These and other publications are listed in the reading list at the end of this present book, *GESTALTING ADDICTION.*

The flawed gestalt AHA
can and all too frequently does
take us down a wrong path.

Just turn on the evening news. Watch and hear so many talking heads reporting, reciting, specific details of news yet rather regularly filling in gaps in available information—and or (mis)interpreting available information. They are frequently (inadvertently I assume) reporting inaccurate summaries of what has been said or has taken place. They are thus completing a picture (of an already incomplete or flawed picture) for us. I have even seen talking heads have direct quotes of individuals posted on the television screen while these talking heads are telling us that so and so has said something so and so has clearly not said.

If you, Readers, ask what this has to do with treating addiction, and or with gestalt therapy or gestalt theory, stay tuned. Here, let me just note that all too many emotional and behavioral patterns such as problem addictions are activated and re-activated over and over in response to inaccurate or at least incomplete perceptions or emotions regarding oneself or "people" or surrounding "events" or "triggers."

In fact, I have come to feel, in my work with several thousand addicted persons over several decades, that the form completion process, the gestalt, while a necessary brain function, can grow more and more what I call *infected by the problem addiction itself.*[9]

---

[9] See the chapters on the "addicted" brain's *attentional bias* that supports its addiction, found in *TRANSCENDING ADDICTION, Second Edition,* and in the *Psychobiological Profiles* volume of the *INTERNATIONAL COLLECTION ON ADDICTIONS.* See reading list at the end of this present book, *GESTALTING ADDICTION.*

SO, WHAT PICTURE DO WE COMPLETE?

Referring to one of the definitional quotes I offer at the start of this book, I appreciate that the author of the *Dune Series*, Frank Herbert, wrote of what he called the "Babel Problem," the label he gave to the "**omnipresent dangers of achieving wrong combinations from accurate information**." I would of course add that there may also be wrong combinations or conclusions, *flawed gestalt AHAs*, achieved based on INaccurate information, as per the various **dysfunctional form completion processes** I refer to in other publications,[10] what I herein define as being:

INFECTED GESTALTS.

We have all heard the phrase, "jumping to the wrong conclusion." I am suggesting that frequently the wrong conclusion (such as in the case of an **incorrect or distorted AHA reactivating the problem addiction pattern/cycle**) is jumped to as a result of an **infected gestalt**. This infected gestalt can take the form of a distorted or incorrectly activated impulse response such as what I tell my clients can be a …

relapse reflex.

---

[10] Refer to previous footnote about more of my work regarding attentional bias and various brain functions affected by addictions and other conditions, even by what I define elsewhere as simple **preference tendencies**.

SO,
WHAT PICTURE DOES
THE PROBLEM ADDICTION COMPLETE?

I see everywhere around and within us evidence of our brain's programming to not only overlook, but to allow, even to generate, such infected gestalts. This can be the problem addiction program at work. Out of the drive of the problem addiction pattern to sustain itself, to survive, this invasive pattern can be generating cognitive and emotional perceptions and sensations and distortions of these (with resulting problem addicted behaviors) that support its control over its host, over us.

The **trigger-craving-use pattern of (drug/alcohol) addiction builds to (falls into) the trapping double binded lose-lose infected gestalt of the relapse pull into the use of the drug again.** Right there, in the brain's move to relapse, is an **addiction-supporting impulse** generated by an infected gestalt. To reveal the work of invasive addiction programming within us, we must call this addiction programming out of the shadows of our sub- and un-conscious, so that we can consciously address it. (See *Part Six* of this book, where I further discuss, even gestalt, this process.)

ONCE WE LOOK

Once we look at how we "know" what we know, how we see any larger picture, the truth or at least accuracy itself begins to fade as a standard, an absolute. So, when we draw a conclusion, proceed based on what we think we see, feel, or know, when we form a whole picture or a whole circle, we may be doing so out of an incomplete or even damaged or infected (even addicted) perception, picture, or circle. We must always keep in mind how tenuous, even infected, may be the addiction program's gestalt, its distorted figure (or feeling) completion (or conclusion, or craving-

40

use-response) process. So much of problem addiction patterning reveals such…

infected processing.

For example, persons addicted to drugs have shown strong attentional bias[11] toward their "drug/s of choice" as well as toward related objects such as paraphernalia, and even items, events, persons, emotions being viewed as "triggers" for craving/relapse sensations, even relapse itself. Even the sense of what "triggers" craving for, and (re)use of, a drug of addiction, is the work of the addiction programming to identify particular persons, places, things, or feelings as triggers. The problem addiction programming seeks triggers to continue to hold the program's host (us and our brains) in the addiction pattern.

THE WHOLE
GREATER THAN SUM OF PARTS
DICTUM

Of course the whole is greater than the sum of its parts. I do not question this. The whole is the whole, not just its components. A bag of apples is a bag of apples, not simply apple #1 then apple #2 and so on. The group of apples in the bag has its own characteristics as a group in addition to the characteristics of the bag, and of each individual apple, even the air, any insects, any sprays on the apples, etc. within that bag.

So this whole we see, perceive, is a complex entity of its own. This may be more obvious to us when we think of a crowd as not simply person #1 then person #2 and so on. Crowds take on lives of their

---

[11] See the volume, *Psychobiological Profiles*, of the *INTERNATIONAL COLLECTION ON ADDICTION*.

own. And a crowd in an environment (such as weather, any crowd control agents, the purpose of the gathering, etc.) has characteristics affected by that environment as well as so many other characteristics.

This "whole is greater than the sum of its parts" dictum will likely remain forever true for us, as will the questions I see this dictum raises for us:

Do we ever see (or sense or feel or know) the whole picture? Can we ever see (or sense or feel or know) the whole picture? Is what we see (or sense or feel or know) what we see (or sense or feel or know) or what our brain, in an infected gestalt and other partial and even deceptive perception, tells us we see (sense, feel, and know)?

While I have discussed these and related questions in great depth in other books,[12] it is on the following pages of this present book, *GESTALTING ADDICTION*, that I delve into this matter as it relates to: what addiction is, and what gestalt itself is or can be in this process of understanding ourselves and our addictions.

EXPERIENCE
AFFECTS
THE GESTALT

I say that perception takes place in both the micro (neural for example) and macro (physical, social, environmental) contexts of

---

[12] Again, see reading list at the end of this book for titles such as *OVERRIDING THE EXTINCTION SCENARIO* and *TRANSCENDING ADDICTON*. Also see *UNVEILING THE HIDDEN INSTINCT* for a more philosophical and creative view.

experience. At all levels, environment and context have impact. For example, externally induced trauma (such as war and or disaster related PTSD) can register internally, deep down on the neural level, sometimes priming automatic responses to triggers long after the traumatic event occurs (responses such as fight or flight or freeze, and effects such as flashback, startle reflex, etc.). This is a loud example of environment affecting deep neural processes and their perceptual gestalts.

WE ARE
CONSTANTLY
PROCESSING

During our waking and even sleeping hours, we are constantly processing and responding to our ongoing experience/s within our environment/s. Our thoughts, feelings, behaviors, all reflect this. Of course, we have deep and necessary programming enabling our brain to automatically respond to stimuli as rapidly as possible to protect ourselves from actual or possible danger, at times as rapidly as within the 200 to 500 *milli*second range.

We also have brain programming to consciously think and feel our ways through situations, to respond to stimuli a little more slowly, after at least a few seconds (or more) of **conscious consideration**. (This is part of what I help clients learn to do more and more of, in the *Going Conscious Process* I teach them, introduced in the chapters of *Part Six*).

BEING TRAPPED IN
DANGEROUS
NO EXIT (DOUBLE BIND)
PATTERNS OF PROBLEM ADDICTION

Where we have perhaps stumbled most, even at times suffered most, is in our impulse control and automatic response areas and functions. This has become ever more clear as we have struggled as a species with drug and alcohol (and other behavioral, even nondrug) addictions and patterns. We humans can find ourselves trapped in problematic even dangerous patterns, at times not fully seeing what keeps us trapped there, which is:

**our programming to be
highly addict-able
and to remain
trapped in patterns of addiction.**

Here is where the healthy addiction gestalt, the actual *going conscious*, the sustained insight AHA,[13] and the other processes I describe in this book and other publications, can, with proper, ethical, and highly skilled therapeutic guidance, lead to ongoing corrective (and even healthy) adaptations in perception and then in behavior.

GESTALT AS RELEASE
FROM THE DOUBLE BIND

A great mentor I had the honor to work with, Gregory Bateson, taught us about the double bind, and the release from the double bind. I am forever grateful for his profound insights. I have been excited to connect ever more dots between therapeutic release from the double bind and the gestalt AHA I refer to herein. I say more on the following pages. (See *Chapters 5, 6, and 22, 23, 24, 25, 26,* for example.)

---

[13] What I term the *healthy insight AHA* is a perceptual gestalt leading to the seeing of more and more of the whole, more of oneself as well as more of the addiction itself, *seeing beyond the closed patterns of the problem addiction.*

ABOUT
THIS BOOK

Let me return to overviewing this book. While I herein refer to **principles of perception** and brain processes, as well as other formulations ranging from neuroscientific research to psychological theory to psychological practices such as gestalt therapy, I do not suggest this to be a textbook or research paper in any of these areas. There are plenty of excellent materials available for those who wish to study in depth gestalt theory, gestalt psychology, gestalt therapy, and so on.[14]

What I am doing herein is **offering a new angle on both gestalt and addiction. I am suggesting that the truth about gestalt itself can be reset for new avenues of application, and that the truth about addiction is in the gestalting that addiction (the addiction within us) must now do of itself.**

ON PART ONE

I open this book in *Part One: About This Book*, with the brief note to Readers regarding the powers at work in the outer world, in the treatment and theory fields, and the powers at work in the inner world, deep in the mind (and its body) where addiction itself lives. Speaking truth to these powers must be done (*Chapter 1*).

Next, I offer this introductory overview chapter (*Chapter 2*), where I share my thinking regarding the fields of addiction, addiction treatment, and addiction-related therapy, as well as gestalt as a

---

[14] See for example, the excellent and in depth overview provided by Stephanie Sabar, MSW, LCSW in "What's a gestalt?" *Gestalt Review* 17(1):6-34, 2013.

concept and an AHA, offering an avenue for seeing more about ourselves and our clients, our and their addictions and co-addictions.

I then include a chapter (*Chapter 3*) sharing some background to my writing this book. There I delve into further understanding both addiction and gestalt. I discuss the matter of *gestalting addiction*, what I mean by this, how powerful gestalt can be, what great care must be taken with gestalt techniques, and how speaking these truths herein has so many dimensions.

ON PART TWO

In the process of sharing my thoughts on what I see as being the difficult, even dangerous, double binding[15] nature of addiction, I move into **Part Two: Toward Gestalting Addiction.** *Part Two* opens with what I frame as the question of the hour, the **insight gestalt**, the AHA itself (*Chapter 4*). I explain how central this pivotal mind (both emotional and cognitive) event can be in addiction and other treatments. I ask: What is this AHA, how is it generated, how can this AHA be powerful (and its positives sustained) in addiction therapy contexts?

From there, I discuss the powerful (or at least potentially powerful) relationship between the gestalt AHA and gestalt learning, as here is where the benefits of an AHA can be learned, sustained. I refer again to Gregory Bateson and note his Theory of Learning (*Chapter 5*). I see that the AHA and the higher level/s of learning can indeed be concurrent in, or even key in the moments of, the most profound AHA's.

---

[15] See *Chapter 5* of this book where I discuss the work of Gregory Bateson, for example, his levels of learning and gestalt or deutero learning.

I offer my thinking in the spirit of adding new dimensions to gestalt theory and therapy (*Chapter 6*). This discussion builds further my message that the *sustained* AHA I see as so intrinsic in this *gestalting addiction* I am describing herein can (when facilitated by adept therapists) facilitate profound insight, learning, *and* behavior change.

ON PART THREE

Next, in *Part Three: Faces of Gestalt*, I move deeper into this inquiry into addiction and gestalt, calling for **addiction itself to reveal more about itself, even to gestalt itself**. I dig deeper into **gestalt, its theory and psychology**. I tie **assertive confrontation practices** into some uses (perhaps mis-uses or misunderstandings) of gestalt and its derivatives (*Chapters 7* and *8*). I consider some of the basic tenets of foundational gestalt theory to place this discussion in context, to both include and reach beyond these (*Chapter 8*).

ON PART FOUR

In *Part Four: Looking Beyond Known Addiction for the Actual Addiction*, I look at **denial as a factor** influencing the use of confrontation in the treatment of addiction (confrontation which may or may not be useful in effectively addressing addiction) (*Chapters 9* and *10*). I also talk about the matters of: addiction working its way deeply into **our neural networks**; and, the *gestalting addiction* I define herein as a process of calling addiction itself out of hiding within us (*Chapter 12*).

Note: It is in *Chapter 11* that I include a comment regarding the medically assisted and psychedelically assisted treatments of addiction, and their relevance to this discussion on *gestalting addiction*. I advocate for great and highly informed care in administering both psychopharmacological (medically assisted treatment of addiction or MAT) and psychedelic approaches (the use of hallucinogens, etc. in treatments of addiction and of other conditions, what I describe as PAT). I also strongly differentiate between the various MATs (medically assisted treatments) and the various PATs (psychedelically assisted treatments). And, I call for far greater research on not only short term effects but also on **long term effects upon the brain (the lasting brain changing effects) of such treatments.**

We are indeed talking about brain changes here, externally induced (via psychotropic Rx medications and or psychedelics, hallucinogens, etc.) changes in the brain, changes that are generally irreversible and may have long term unforeseen effects. As these are treatments being administered to "treat" addiction which itself can cause irreversible brain changes, those administering MATs and PATs must proceed with great care. I am already seeing, now for several years, clients coming to me to get help with the effects of MATs and PATs they have been or are in the process of being administered by others, such as licensed (and yes, some unlicensed) professionals, practitioners, and spiritual guides. So, while there are persons whose lives may be made better by MAT and or PAT interventions, there are others who do not benefit and are even harmed. Again, no one general statement can be made regarding effectiveness of MATs and PATs, and these forms of assistance must proceed, conducted by highly trained experts, on case by case bases.

ON PART FIVE

Part Five: Unveiling Addiction for What the Addiction Is opens with the notion of what I describe herein and elsewhere as **inhabiting,** the **addiction inhabiting us on all levels,** ranging from macro levels such as societal on down to the neural and synaptic micro levels (an **inhabiting** I have felt to be taking place in so many of my addicted clients) (*Chapter 13*).

Then I return to the matter of addiction revealing to us who it is, showing its face and actual nature, gestalting itself. What we see in looking so closely at addiction is the duality and double bind so inherent in addiction, and **how very addict-able we are wired to be**[16] (*Chapter 14*). Looking this closely, ever more is revealed about addiction, such as what I call the **identified addict** (*Chapter 15*). Can we really stop ourselves from becoming addicted? Is there actual survival value in our addict-ability? How far has the human brain run off course, awry? (*Chapter 16*).

ON PART SIX

Part Six: Unveiling, Gestalting, and Confronting the Addiction in Therapy shares ideas, processes, and suggestions regarding how psychotherapists, and other clinicians and practitioners, can work with the concepts and material I present in this book. *Part Six* highlights the paradoxical double bind in life and in problem addiction, and therapeutic aspects of working with this *paradoxical nature of addiction* (*Chapters 17* and *18*, and all through the chapters of *Part Six*.) *Part Six* asks: Can we move our addiction tendencies and patterns ever further out of our sub- and even un- conscious levels, right up to our conscious level/s where we can begin to effectively address these? Every chapter in *Part Six* is part of the process I have developed and tested over years in

---

[16] I have elsewhere discussed in great detail our programming to form patterns, habits, even to become addicted, and the survival value of this programming as it allows us to form healthy patterns, habits, and addictions. Clearly our brains are running awry where this programming can also turn to self harming patterns and addictions. I define this programming as our **addict-ability** in other publications such as in the chapters on the brain in *OVERRIDING THE EXTINCTION SCENARIO, Part One*.

working with persons dealing with problem addictions to alcohol/drugs and to non-drug behaviors and emotional patterns.

After opening *Part Six* with a discussion of **gestalting the paradox of addiction** (*Chapter 17*), I turn to a discussion of the **power of paradox** itself and its relevance in working with problem addiction (*Chapter 18*). Next I look at what I define as the **four basic stages of our journey**, four stages I have found highly useful in assisting clients in understanding their own processes (*Chapters 19* and *20*). All this is key in the next part of this process I share with my clients, the recognizing and **facing of ingrained problem addiction patterns** (*Chapter 21*). From there I discuss the **undrugging feelings** work I do with clients (*Chapter 22*). All this leads to highlights of both the *Going Conscious* and the *AHA Processes* I have designed in my work with clients (*Chapters 23* and *24*), and the *Gestalting Addiction Processes* I conduct with my clients and teach in my workshops (*Chapters 24, 25,* and *26*). I conclude with a discussion of navigating what I describe as the *emotional terrain* in *gestalting addiction* (*Chapter 26*).

TRUTH ABOUT US

The conclusion to this book is titled, *The Truth About Us*. I certainly hope that ideas unveiled here in this book serve as not the last word but rather as seminal, an invitation to ever greater realizations and AHAs, truths about us, our minds and brains, our programmings, our addictions, our **selves**.

3
Some Background

A brief note of background here: Early in my career, one of the books I wrote addressed the use of a form of therapy, what was being called "gestalt therapy," in treating (drug/alcohol) addiction. I recall that book project well: my working word by word, line by line, through long transcripts of numerous group therapy sessions conducted by a therapist in an addiction treatment program; my working to give readers a sense of form, structure, and theory in that particular variation of gestalt therapy.

TO THIS DAY:
UNFINISHED THERAPY

Over the years, I hear from some of the participants in those and similar group therapy sessions. Some contact me for information and or therapy when, after all these years, they find themselves seeking to do more work on their addictions, and or wanting to better understand themselves, their life choices, even what it was they had experienced in earlier therapy sessions conducted by other therapists. Many of these persons are addressing potentially active or recently active (or recently reactivated) forms of what they tell me they have come to describe as "life long drug, alcohol, and other addictions."

Some of these persons recall their earlier gestalt therapy experiences where they were, as they say, "opened up to what was going on deep inside," and or "opened up, but not helped to heal the wounds I found so deep inside," and or "given what seemed in the moment a great experience, but one I couldn't make sense of or use afterward," and or "made to cry a lot which was a release for a while. But after I left, the pain continued, came back more intensely now, years later."[17]

Others have said, "That experience stayed with me, and all these years later, I get what it was about. I'm ready for it now that I have lived so many more years." Some have said, "It's like that therapy was a placeholder, something I can go back to now. I am glad I've lived long enough to continue that work."

Years later, some of the participants in those earlier gestalt therapy sessions are talking about both the intensity of their previous gestalt therapy experiences, and in many cases, the need for long term follow on (far more than a year or two or three), as the questions, the impact, the need for further work, even in some cases the trauma (even the trauma of the therapy itself) is being experienced so much later.

IMPORTANT
LONG TERM IMPLICATIONS

Psychotherapists conducting highly intensive, emotionally incisive, gestalt (as well as other forms of deep) therapy (for example, gestalt therapy with persons who are experiencing problem addictions) will do well to truly recognize the potential long term implications of such work. I advise psychotherapists

---

[17] Frequently, in an addiction treatment/therapy program/experience, follow-on therapy is advised. However, extremely long term (several decades of) follow-on therapy is rarely if ever advised. Addiction treatment/therapy graduates/participants are generally encouraged to join Twelve Step and or other peer group programs (which for many has proven immensely valuable advice). Such decisions are, for the most part, left to the clients/patients.

doing such work to inform clients and others participating that there can be long term (and frequently unforeseen) effects of intensive psychological work.[18]

Interestingly enough, while gestalt therapy includes in its repertoire various "unfinished business" processes and exercises that assist participants in exploring and releasing "stuffed away" emotions and issues—the gestalt therapy itself may create other unfinished business in these same persons. I call this *unfinished therapy* and or *unfinished gestalt therapy*.

Additionally, addiction rarely arrives solo in addiction-related therapy or treatment. Co-occurring conditions are common. Where there is co-occurring trauma, the clinician conducting gestalt or other intensive therapy must be aware of the possibility, even reality, of **revictimization**.

When engaged in gestalt therapy processes such as the common exercises, "unfinished business" and unpacking "emotional baggage," it is **essential the clinician know that what may be unfinished or packed away in a client's emotional baggage are traumas and also triggers for reliving past traumas. This can mean that the client can be revictimized during therapy, retraumatized right during the gestalt (or other form of) therapy itself.** I therefore

---

[18] While, for the most part, it is up to the client to choose to or not to continue on in therapy over time, the psychotherapist can be proactive in explaining to the client (at the start of, in deciding to proceed with, and then again during, the intensive therapy experience) that: (a) such deep work may call itself (back) to the forefront of the client's mind at some point in the future; (b) it is important for the client to take responsibility for later check-in and follow-on therapy on an ongoing basis; and, (c) the client should continue to remain aware of this over time.

strongly suggest that psychotherapists' training address matters of *traumatic therapy,* and of *revictimization in therapy.*

POWER TOOLS
DO NOT ALWAYS WORK

I have frequently taught therapy techniques and processes to clinicians, students, and interns. Again and again, I find myself saying, "Simply because you have learned some powerful techniques, simply because you now have these *power tools* in your possession, does not mean you utilize these at will or without great care." I say this advice is essential in any psychotherapy training being conducted.

Handing a surgeon a powerful surgical tool to cut into a patient is not enough, and at times may be too much, too powerful, too dangerous. Once that surgeon cuts into the patient, a new wound or at least incision is in essence created. Sure, this may allow the surgeon to identify, perhaps to remove or repair or otherwise address, problems "inside" that patient. However, this surgeon must know what to do once in there, how to proceed with great care, and when complete, how to close the surgical wound made so that the patient moves on in a healthy and safe way.

I offer similar advice to clinicians performing psychotherapy. The goal is not simply to dig in deep and let the client bleed emotions out into the room. Certainly, some minor or even major (yet frequently only momentary or time limited) relief may be felt by some clients when unexpressed or unrecognized (or suppressed or denied) feelings are discovered and expressed.

However, this is not in itself the end of treatment. Yes, yes, yes, this may look like and sound like treatment and or therapy. Tears may be shed, shouting may be done, things may be hit or thrown.[19] However, the drama in itself is not therapy, and does not necessarily heal or help without more in depth work before, during, and for quite some time following this drama. Again: drama is not in itself therapy. And, drama in itself for the sake of drama can at times even be *counter therapeutic* (something it appears some practitioners either do not fully recognize or admit).

DOWNLOADING PAIN

Among the most dramatic events I observed when writing that early book on gestalt therapy were: participants, in that case men, being told to hold other men down so that intense rage could be expressed what was said to be safely; chairs and other items being broken as padded bats ("boffers" that were padded for safety) were repeatedly slammed against these chairs (at times where photos of family members or others were placed); wailing and screaming into pillows to allow for emotional release; and other elements of what were viewed as central components of that particular form of gestalt therapy.

----

[19] This is not to criticize **psychodrama** (developed by Jacob Moreno), versions of which are frequently applied in gestalt (and other) therapy. This is to say that drama in therapy must be understood for its value as well as its short and long term ramifications (which clients should be told about). Psychodrama itself is used in both clinical and non-clinical settings. In clinical settings, psychodrama is a psychotherapy that can address dysfunctional attachments, emotional trauma, abuse, and other issues. Psychodrama has clients act out past or current events during which the client can express/develop her or his identity, can mirror her or himself, can engage in role reversal work dramatizing interactions and emotions regarding others, etc. When applied in any intensive psychotherapy process (such as gestalt therapy can be), care must be taken to address possible new traumatization and re-traumatization of clients undergoing these dramatic re-enactments.

DRAMATIC THERAPY
MUST BE MONITORED AFTERWARD

To this day, I hear from some of the participants in those and other groups that:

> "The *drama* was unforgettable, and it made a great impression on me. But after the drama wore off, I felt I was left with a hole inside, nothing to fill it with, the need for help with what I had just experienced. I still feel this hole inside sometimes."

> "I realize all these years later that the therapy itself was stressful, that what was going on did not end up making a lasting difference in my addiction to drugs."

> "It was a great release at first, a real upper, but after I left that therapy, there was a let down feeling, a real downer. Now days when I remember that therapy experience, I feel real emotional and confused and don't know what to do."

> "It's like that therapy experience was a high and then afterward, I came down from that high again, crashed, like I do when I come down from my drugs. Now, these days, I feel like therapy is a roller coaster ride just like using drugs is. So I don't know what to do about getting help when stuff from those old therapy sessions comes up again, and it always does."

Reports of after effects, sometimes these effects appearing years after the therapy was engaged in, are important feedback for all who conduct intensive psychotherapy, in this case, intensive gestalt therapy. In an ideal world, experiences with such deep reaching intensive psychotherapy can be attended to in both the short term and the long term. Clearly, this cannot always be done, as many clients do not continue in therapy for years, even decades, let alone stay with the same therapist.

It is therefore essential that psychotherapists make clients aware (up front) of the: (a) potentially positive and even life changing effects of deep work, yes; and, (b) possible long term effects (memories, re-livings, new "stuff coming up years later," etc.) of this work; and, (c) the importance of knowing when to see a therapist again, what signs and effects to look for over the years.

CONTINUING THE QUESTIONING

As have many of my colleagues, I have had ongoing opportunity to contribute to the development, refinement, and even correction of gestalt and other psychotherapy techniques. I have also had the opportunity to see the flaws in earlier thinking. I have seen limiting and even flawed assumptions being applied by many previous and present leaders and practitioners as they impose their views and models on clients and patients. While I see how well intentioned so much of this work has been and is, I also see a clear and present need for more informed use of powerful psychotherapeutic tools such as those found in some gestalt therapy. (Again, note that while these tools can be immensely valuable and useful, even life changing, these techniques must be administered and conducted with great awareness on the part of the psychotherapist.)

Of course, as is true in many fields, knowledge and science have dramatically progressed in recent decades, so previous practices may likely improve or at least mature. However, there has been and may still remain, at least to some degree, an implicit mandate, a largely unspoken dictum, not to question previous or present leaders in addiction treatment, psychotherapy, gestalt, and related fields.

Still, I find it is the questioning, the looking for further insight and understanding, that moves us forward in all fields, and of course in addiction treatment and therapy. Indeed, as a result of questioning givens, numerous valuable new perspectives and practices have emerged.

DEVELOPING NEW APPROACHES

Over the years, I have had the opportunity to develop my thinking and practice in gestalt and adaptations of gestalt, as well as in numerous other forms of therapy and treatment, and have developed several additional forms and processes.

The matters of: general use of gestalt therapy; and, forms of addiction-related therapy drawing upon the thinking behind gestalt therapy; have nevertheless remained a point of inquiry for me. I have found myself reviewing and rethinking the practice, application, and possible uses of gestalt therapy and its elements, as well the relevance of aspects of gestalt theory, gestalt learning, and gestalt psychology.

Moreover, given my ongoing research in ever advancing areas such as neuroscience of addiction and trauma, I have been looking deeper, behind the therapy. I have been examining concepts such as underlying neural mechanisms of the form completion gestalt, and of the gestalt experience (as in the gestalt AHA). This neural mechanism based "brain science," as some call it, has driven me to form new views of addiction itself, views and approaches I have developed and introduce in this and other books. (See *Part Six*.)

In the years since I wrote that early book reviewing one therapist's application of gestalt therapy in addiction treatment, I have observed and studied hundreds of group therapy processes and sessions, many calling themselves gestalt therapy, or employing gestalt approaches without naming (or in some cases even knowing) these as such.

I have also designed and conducted my own version of what may be called gestalt therapy, or what I call *gestalt*ING *therapy*. **This is something markedly different from what I observed and wrote about years ago. This offers a different perspective with a different unit of analysis:**

> *I first define the addiction as the "problem" addiction. I then shift the definition of the "problem addiction" away from the individual client and to the invasive programming, the problem addiction patterning.*

In my gestaltING addiction therapy (which I detail in *Part Six*), the **unit of analysis is** *the programming inhabiting the client, the addiction patterning itself*. In guiding this metaphor forward, led by the client him or her SELF (depending on the client's readiness to engage in this process), this confrontation with the addiction program ITself becomes a far more client propelled approach, one allowing and promoting a more in depth gestaltING, a deeper therapy process, an incisive process designed to encourage ongoing (and truly sustainable) attitudinal and behavioral insights, understandings, and changes. (Refer to *Part Six*, all chapters, especially *Chapters 22, 24, 25*, and *26*.)

SEEING ADDICTION FOR WHAT IT IS

What I want to bring forward and make explicit, is what I call the …

voice of addiction itself:

addiction calling us to

**see what addiction actually is,
what addiction is actually telling us about itself.**

On these pages, I share my thinking with other professionals, as well as with clients, students, and other lay readers, all of whom I believe deserve to hear the observations and truths I share herein – and deserve to…

**listen to
addiction itself
speaking truth to its own power.**

QUESTIONING
POWERS AND PARADIGMS

Questioning previous and present models and practices can be useful, even essential. Yet, doing so is not always welcomed. It is not always easy to speak truth to power, or even to question power, yet this is a path I and many others have followed much of our lives. It is essential we question the power and paradigm structures in health, mental health, and behavioral health fields, including in addiction treatment and therapy.

While we are so doing, let's be ever more aware of the silent yet powerful programming we have always within us: that of addiction itself and its deeply implanted self-preserving self-perpetuating patterning.

The power of this addiction programming can be utilized well (in generating the positive patterning so essential to our functioning, living, and survival). This powerful programming can also be turned on us—or better stated, *turn itself on us, turn against us and our well-being.* The more we see this programming for what it is, and for the risks to us of carrying this essential yet dangerous *addict-ability* programming, the more ready we are to catch this programming running awry. This requires we adjust our understanding of what addiction is, which is the intention of this book, *GESTALTING ADDICTION*.

QUESTION THE PARADIGM

**It is essential we
question the addiction paradigm,
even speak truth to addiction itself.**

I have continued to question practices, models, theories, and paradigms, an ongoing questioning I believe is most necessary. Of course, questioning givens, traditions, theories, other persons working in these fields (some of whom view themselves as being the leaders in these fields; some even seeing themselves as leaders we should not question), questioning power structures within and of encompassing fields, can be challenging. *I know first hand that the response to questioning and challenging can be intense, and frequently takes place behind the scenes, is even stealth, yet very present.* Still, this challenging I write of here is frequently key in the essential process of speaking truth to what assumes and demands the role of power.

Yes, there are even powers in fields such as addiction treatment. As you will see on the following pages, I have a somewhat different view of addiction. I call addiction itself out of the shadows, want us to be clear about what addiction itself is, and hence to rethink (or at least fine tune) even the best of the definitions, therapies, and treatments of what is being called addiction. Note that what you read on the following pages is not a discussion of the various forms of addiction treatment (which I and others offer in other publications). Rather, this book, *GESTALTING ADDICTION*, offers a distinct, perhaps slightly revolutionary, expansion of the concept of addiction itself.

POWER?

A note about power. Questioning power is essential. For some, this power is a belief or a theory. For others, this power is a person and or even an apparent (or self defined) leader, yes. For still others, this power may be a behavior, or a drug, or some other focus, center, or object of an addiction.

**This power
is the power that
patterns have over
the brain and mind,
and the power
the brain and mind give patterns,
including patterns of addiction.**

Reader, whatever form of power you may at some point be (or are already) challenging, standing up to this power can be demanding, yes, and also rewarding. And, where there is an addictive (and or co-addictive) pattern demanded by this power (by this **power pattern**), your recognizing this patterning can be key in breaking free of this power (**power pattern**) itself, and in overcoming any...

**addiction to itself this
power (power pattern)
demands.**

VARIOUS LEVELS OF ADDICTIONS

I have spent much of my career addressing the matter of addiction. In so doing, I have come to see **addiction as a state of mind and consciousness, a patterning, a program being patterned into us**. I find that, in its most obvious form, addiction is what I define as being *explicit* addiction. Yet, as many clinicians have done in their own ways, I have wanted to address the underpinnings of addiction, what I find to be the actual addiction. I have therefore labeled the obvious addictions *explicit*, yet the more hidden or subtle addictions or elements of addictions, *implicit*, as in *implicit* addiction. Clearly, most professional settings continue to address explicit addictions such as alcohol addiction, and or other drug/substance addiction (or what is frequently called chemical dependence), and this is important work. Yet, I can see there is more to address – and that it is time to do this addressing....

Behind every explicit addiction is a host of far less visible, implicit, underlying addictions. Addiction is so very complex that what we see when we choose to face, treat, define addiction is not what we get. Even when we believe we are seeing and treating a particular addiction, we are all too frequently addressing what appears on the surface, just the tip of the iceberg.

Treating only the explicit addiction/s
and only the explicit co-occurring condition/s,
misses far too much,
and too often misses the point.

INSIDIOUS?

My decades of work in the psycho-social and consciousness fields have allowed me to see the human struggle, as well as the human mind, personality, and spirit, up against problem addictions, right there striving to survive amidst very troubled, often...

insidious
patterns.

ON SPEAKING TRUTH

Decades into my work with the human mind, and with the people coming to me for help with their human minds, I have seen that questioning professional givens, pushing accepted boundaries, taking research and practice to new levels, is useful *and even necessary*.

Indeed, we must learn well what we are being told is the rule, the theory, the dominant paradigm. We must learn this so well that we see right through the power of this dominance, see through to the reality this dominance too often denies and demands we not see:

THE TRUTH ABOUT ADDICTION.

Part Two:

Toward
Gestalting Addiction

Dr. Angela®

"Can This Be Me?"

4
The Gestalt AHA

Gestalt is so many things to so many persons working in so many fields. Yet, there is at least an implied constant in views of gestalt: **the law of closure: form completion**, the brain's tendency to complete a partial picture, to "see" (or, as I prefer to say, to tell us it is seeing, sensing, feeling, knowing) more of the whole picture than the fragments we are able to actually "see" show us.

THE AHA
IN GESTALTING ADDICTION

This chapter, in fact this book, is about powerful experiences of seeing, feeling, sensing more about ourselves and our realities, about our experiences. Ideally, knowing more about ourselves can make a difference in our lives.

This is about our clients (and ourselves) experiencing not only brief, but ideally lasting, *shifts in awareness: form completion of their (and our) perceptions, emotions, cognitions*. I find that sustained shifts in and expansions of awareness are of great value in psychotherapy, including in gestalt therapy, and central in the *Gestalting Addiction Processes* I share in this book.

What is essential in this *gestalting addiction* I am defining herein is understanding how to guide others such as clients (and yes, ourselves) in what I describe as this *form completion gestalt*, this *gestalt AHA process*, and in sustaining the positives of this process. I address what I describe as the *gestalt event* and its **AHA** here, at this early point in this book, as this can be a powerful factor in *gestalting addiction.*

LEARNING MATTERS
IN GESTALTING ADDICTION

The *gestalting of addiction* I define in this book maintains that generating and then sustaining the AHA, the *form completion insight,* is key. Throughout this book, I note that when *actual learning* takes place, powerful insight can be sustained (as per *Chapter 5* on gestalt learning and *Chapters 17, 18,* and *19* on stages of our journey). This *actual learning* can generate sustained cognitive, emotional, and behavioral shifts, changes so essential in moving through and beyond problem addiction patterns (patterns of addiction to the range of drugs, alcohols, behaviors, emotions, mind sets, and more). *Actual* positive learning *actually* involves *actual* positive brain changes: brain cells change shape, new synaptic activity occurs, new neural activity patterns develop and trigger positive cognitive, emotional, and behavioral changes.[20]

GESTALT AHA MATTERS
IN GESTALTING LEARNING

To stimulate or *gestalt* the learning (see *Chapter 5*) that can *sustain* the insight, a deep understanding of the AHA is essential. The gestalt AHA involves understanding and generating what I call the *AHA function.* Recognizing this AHA function also involves knowing and reaching beyond standard definitions of the AHA. In my work, an AHA is in itself a gestalt. To wit, the AHA is in essence a sort of form completion, a completion of what is always a partial

---

[20] University of Pittsburg. *How the brain changes when mastering a new skill: Research reveals new neural activity patterns that emerge with long term learning.* Science Daily. June 10, 2019.

picture (of what is seen, sensed, felt, perceived), as there is always more to see, sense, feel, perceive than we do, as we never have the entirely "whole" picture.

BRIEF INSIGHT AHA

Before moving into this discussion of the AHA, I note that, what is generally (in several fields) defined as an AHA, a sudden realization, can be quite valuable. However, I do find that the value can be best realized when the AHA, what I call the *insight AHA*, is sustained, in what I call an actual *elevation AHA*, an elevation of the learning and understanding that can result from AHAs and their potentially powerful realizations. (See *Chapter 19* where I define the insight and the elevation stages, also *Chapter 5* where I discuss elevating the awareness in gestalt learning.)

SUSTAINED ELEVATION AHA

This *elevation AHA sustains the insight* (as in *Chapter 19*), and is where cognitive, emotional, behavioral, and other shifts and changes can result -- and in turn have the highest likelihood of being further sustained. (See *Part Six* for further discussion on encouraging, identifying, and applying *insight and elevation*, sustaining the AHA, in therapeutic contexts.)

NOTE ON
FALSE AHAs

This discussion must also address what I have seen to be a *false AHA* (what I also describe as an *infected gestalt)*. I have found this to be a function the addicted brain (actually, the problem addiction pattern's brain programming) applies to hold its hosts – to hold *us* -- in place, in the pattern of addiction, and even to expand its power, its problem addiction pattern. It is therefore essential we watch for and recognize unhealthy **problem addiction driven form** completions, infected problem addiction driven perceptions, false or infected gestalts. I have come to recognize the invasive problem addiction pattern as a *condition affecting what we "see" or believe we "see" (sense, feel, know)*. Indeed, in order to sustain itself, this problem addiction pattern moves itself into dominance over us, including over what we "see" as being our reality, our needs, our options. I return to this matter later in this chapter.***

RECOGNIZE
HEALTHY FORM COMPLETIONS
AND LASTING AHAs

In developing this *Gestalting Addiction Process,* I see authentic form completion gestalts and related AHAs as the shiftings of understanding and awareness to higher levels of perception and thought organization.

Of course, not all AHAs are only momentary. Some are achieved more consciously, or at least their "roll out" and "aftermath" processes are more consciously sustained. (This can take place when we are aware of what an AHA is and how to maximize its value to us. This is part of the *Going Conscious Process* I offer in the chapters of *Part Six.*)

Again note, in *gestalting addiction,* where the AHA is a momentary or brief insight, a glimpse, its shift in awareness may not hold. Where this AHA and its shift are *consciously sustained,* then there is an actual lasting shift. Here is where a *transformative form of learning* -- an *elevation* of knowledge, awareness, and resulting behavior, can take place. (See *Chapter 19,* and all chapters in *Part Six.*) Generating this shifting is the *gestalting* I refer to herein.

In that addressing, taking some control over, even seeking to overcome, problem addiction patterning requires sustained shifts in understanding, awareness, and perception in order to bring about significant positive behavior change, this *gestalting* can be quite useful in addressing problem addiction.

Here is where the psychotherapeutic facilitation, even generation, of sustained AHAs (gestalt learnings and their resulting elevations) in gestalt processes, can be a powerful element in *GESTALTING ADDICTION*. (See for examples, *Chapters 5, 24,* and *25.*)

QUESTIONING
THE NOTION OF THE AHA

But what is this AHA we seek? Or do we actually seek AHAs? Do we actually seek AHAs and not realize we do so?

Let's ask all this another way. Do we carry within us the pursuit of greater understanding, the drive to know more, to see what's really going on, to experience a dawning of realization, of "knowing?" In this sense, are we consciously seeking the AHA? Are we also perhaps seeking AHA moments quite subconsciously without consciously realizing we are so doing?

Answers to these questions may in themselves require AHAs. But what, pray tell, is this AHA we have heard so much about? And again, why is the AHA so relevant to this discussion on *gestalting addiction*?

As noted earlier, the AHA can be said to be the core of the gestalt, even the gestalt itself. In essence, the AHA is the closing, gestalting, of the broken circle -- the seeing or revealing of (more of) the whole picture. When sudden, this striking AHA is an insight experience, a (seemingly) sudden realization, what some will call a "Eureka" moment.

As I explain in *Part Six*, when **sustained**, the AHA is an elevated, potentially life changing event, an epiphany with potentially profound, transformative, implications, perhaps even a great AHA.[21]

An elevation, a sustained AHA, can be pivotal in a human life and mind, if recognized for its power, especially if encouraged and guided as central in processes of emotional and behavioral adjustment and change therapies. Of course this means we must understand the AHA, in order to ensure and maximize its positive impact, and the sustainability of this positive impact.

EVERDAY AHAs

Of course, there are minor and major AHAs everywhere within and around us, even in daily life. It is even likely our brains have AHAs (connect data/information or move data/information to another or higher level of organizational complexity) behind the curtain, out of range of our own conscious awareness. [22] Although perhaps never having formally labelled these *unseen subliminal gestalts* as our own personal gestalts, we are quite consciously familiar with many other of our minor and major gestalts: sudden realizations, shifts in knowing, leaps in levels of awareness, the AHA in its many

---

[21] As early as 1907, German psychologist and linguist known for his work in gestalt psychology, Karl Ludwig Buhler, wrote of the *AHA experience*, and published his work on *Facts and problems of the psychology of thought processes*. Buhler described the AHA experience as a "moment in which suddenly the lights come on." [See Stephanie Sabar's article, "What is gestalt?" *Gestalt Review*, 17(1):6-34:2013.] Note: After being detained by the Nazis in 1938, Buhler fled to London in 1940, then to Oslo, then emigrated to the United States where he worked as a professor.

[22] See my further discussions of consciousness and awareness, and of what I term, *aware consciousness*, in UNVEILING THE HIDDEN INSTINCT and also in OVERRIDING THE EXTINCTION SCENARIO, Part One, as listed in reading list on last pages of this present book, GESTALTING ADDICTION.

forms. We talk about and hear about AHAs such as these all the time:

"It just dawned on me...."
"I was about to give up when I realized that...."
"Suddenly it all made sense...."
"And then, I heard a (or my?) voice telling me...."
"I've got it!"

"AHA!"

Sometimes we are fully aware we have just experienced an **AHA**. That flash of understanding races through us. This flash, this insight, is the **AHA moment**. Throughout this book, I add to existing AHA theory that, when sustained through a higher level of knowing, a gestalt learning, the AHA is an elevation: a leap[23] to a higher level of perceiving and thus higher level of experiencing, knowing, learning. We, our mind and brain, suddenly put together data, information, in a different way and see (sense, feel, recognize, know) what has not been seen (sensed, felt, recognized, known) before or seen (sensed, felt, recognized, known) this way before. And we hold on to this new way of "seeing." This is indeed the sustained insight, the *elevation*.[24]

---

[23] This is the *LEAP: light energy action process* I have defined and taught in experiential courses and workshops where professionals and lay persons can experience this thinking, this mind-shifting AHA-like process. See for example the definition of the *LEAP* I offer in *UNVEILING THE HIDDEN INSTINCT*.

[24] Referring to "seeing," I conceptually extend the founding definitions in gestalt theory beyond the domain of visual perception central in original gestalt theory to include other sensory, perceptual, and even emotional awareness-es.

THE AHA
REVEALS
THAT THERE IS
A WAY OUT OF THE

DOUBLE BIND

The solution to a dilemma, problem, or question suddenly comes to mind, flashes into the awareness. A realization takes place. A way out of a double bind, a way out of a seeming no way out situation of not knowing, not seeing, (not having a solution) is seen (or sensed, felt, recognized, known). We are released at least momentarily from a stuck place, a no solution, lose-lose, double bind. This can happen from one moment to the next. Suddenly we "get it." This "grok" experience can be that instantaneous.[25] And, as noted above, we can learn what it means to sustain the value of such an AHA.

BEYOND
SIMPLY
INTUITIVE
OR ANALYTICAL

Although popular explanations of the AHA experience tend to frame the AHA as intuitive as opposed to analytical, the AHA actually pulls from both the intuitive and the analytical functions

---

[25] See the "grok" offered us by science fiction author, Robert Heinlein, in STRANGER IN A STRANGE LAND, referring to an intuitive understanding of something, a merging with the information so as to know it, an absorbing of the information via other than more "mechanical" cognitive processing means.

of the brain. And, while being ignited or propelled by right hemisphere activity, the AHA involves, moves across and through, both the right and left brain hemispheres.

We may require a third category that is neither entirely intuitive nor entirely analytical to better describe the AHA process. Perhaps the AHA is (or can become) in essence a unique brain function. I suggest the AHA can be learned and then further developed, so as to be ever more unique and even consciously generated. (It is likely we can elect our own views of the AHA based upon our own theoretical and philosophical orientations and life experiences, and still learn to generate profound AHAs.)

SO
THIS IS
YOUR BRAIN
ON THE

AHA!

What this thing, this event, this AHA, actually is, how exactly this AHA is generated/initiated, what it is that happens following this AHA, are questions we continue to ask. We do know the AHA can be, sometimes is, highly transformative.[26] However, we are not yet, and perhaps ever, able to measure entirely, precisely, and fully the actual cell by cell, synapse by synapse, brain effects and brain changes taking place during and around the time of *transformative experience*. Nor are we able to identify at that precise granular

---

[26] When something is transformative, it is "causing a major change to something or someone, especially in a way that makes it or them better," as defined by the *Cambridge Dictionary*.

biochemical and synaptic level which AHA might be a positive one, an authentic one, an "UNinfected" one.

Researchers have sought to identify specific brain activity during an AHA or moment of insight (what some describe as creative insight or epiphany). This makes sense, as it is good to know what the brain is doing leading into and during an AHA. If there is truly something highly valuable in such AHA moments, why not find a way to identify, promote, stimulate, encourage, and replicate these? Just think what we can do if we can generate the flash of inspiration at will. Just think what everyday people such as ourselves might be able to do once we know how to bring about great insights. Why not make this high on our agendas?[27]

THE ASTONISHING AHA FUNCTION

Research is offering a great deal of "insight" into the what I define as the *insight AHA*, what researchers generally define as *the* AHA. For example, researchers are using MRI, EEG, and other

---

[27] Certainly, this is one of the driving factors in related brain research (such as via brain scans, EEGs, and other technological measures) which range from scientific studies of the brain in its "natural state" while processing information/data, to alternative work considering effects of psychoactives including hallucinogens such as LSD. I, however, advocate for as much understanding of what the brain is doing unaided by psychopharmacology (drugs) to first know what the unaided brain itself is indeed doing.

Of course, I do appreciate the scientific endeavor; however, administering psychedelic treatment (or medicine or intervention, depending on how this is being described) to study (or treat) a subject's mind/brain may bring with it a host of ethical, medical, and psychological issues that I contend are, for the most part, best left at bay while the deeper research into the unaided brain is *first further solidified*. Refer to *Chapter 11*.

technologies[28] to document subjects' neural activity while they solve problems. Among the profound findings of such research is that …

> **"the brain already knows whether a problem will be solved analytically or through sudden insight, and what's more, the brain knows this an astonishing eight seconds before hand, before the insight."**[29]

What? The brain knows it is going to select, choose to experience, the sudden insight, the AHA option, eight seconds before it does!

So here we are, face to face, with the brain and its directing, choosing to opt into or deny, the AHA option/experience. This suggests that, on some level, likely on the sub- or the un- conscious or both levels, we (our brains) are choosing whether or not to elect the AHA, the more (although not entirely) intuitive (intuitive-analytic) mode of problem solving, or to address the problem in a more cognitive-analytic function type of mode.[30]

---

[28] The MRI (magnetic resonance imaging) uses a magnetic field and computer generated radio waves to generate detailed images of an organ such as the brain. The EEG (electroencephalography) measures the electrical activity of the brain via electrodes that are placed on the scalp.

[29] See for example, *Remote brainwaves predict future 'Eureka' moment.* Science Daily, September 12, 2018.
<< https://www.sciencedaily.com/releases/2008/09/080909095108.htm >>

[30] Elsewhere, I discuss in depth the matter of our brain's programming to control our processes and modes, including our problem solving processes and modes—and to control our *"decisions" regarding (or selecting)* which processes/modes to apply when. See *UNVEILING THE HIDDEN INSTINCT* and *OVERRIDING THE EXTINCTION SCENARIO* on reading list at the end of this present book, *GESTALTING ADDICTION.*

I find this can be a key understanding in psychotherapeutic (gestalt and other) work with clients seeking behavior change assistance, as are many who present problem addictions: The *brain has the option* of addressing a problem primarily emotionally, or to elect between a more cognitive-analytical or more intuitive-analytical approach, or doing something combining these methods in a new way, such as *gestalting addiction* via an intentional, conscious, AHA-generating-and-sustaining process. (See *Part Six* of this book for more on this process.)

THE
TRANSFORMATIVE REASONING
OF THE
INSIGHT AHA

Studies of subjects' brainwaves while these subjects are working on brainteasers indicate that there is a distinct pattern of unconscious neural activity during the "pre-solution process." This neural activity occurs right before an AHA or Eureka moment of actually "seeing" how to solve the problem (the brainteaser problem in this case).

Such studies have found that the right hemisphere of the brain is quite active (although not acting alone) in this transformative problem solving or what has been called "transformative reasoning." The gestalt AHA reasoning process appears to activate increases in right hemisphere activity, and on the surface appears more intuitive than analytical. Yet, the AHA is frequently an analytical sort of Eureka moment. Hence reasoning takes on new meaning in this realm. (The gestalt AHA in itself can be a moment of profound transformative reasoning, and in this, again when consciously sustained, elevated, a minor or even major transformative learning.)

EIGHT SECONDS TO INSIGHT

Following the eight second pre-AHA time period, the subject experiences the AHA. So it is, following waves of unconscious neural activity, that the subject then consciously experiences the AHA. The move from the pre-AHA to the AHA moment has been described as a "quantum leap of understanding with no conscious forewarning," and the moving from "a state of not knowing how to solve a problem to a state of knowing how to solve it."[31] Aided by neuroimaging tools, "cognitive neuroscience of insight" studies suggest that the AHA is a "sudden reorganization of a knowledge representation resulting in a new understanding or solution to a problem."

In general literature and practice, the AHA is usually viewed as being an insight. Again note, what I am sharing in this book is the notion of *sustaining an insight into an elevation*, frequently via gestalt learning (as per *Chapter 5*). I further explain the notion of sustaining insight in later chapters (*Part Six* chapters). Such sustaining of insight can have profound implications in psychotherapy, and in the **gestalting addiction** psychotherapy and processes I introduce in *Part Six*.

Clinical psychology addresses insight in various ways, largely viewing insight as self awareness. Cognitive psychology research was preceded by earlier gestalt studies which distinguished between insight and analysis. This differentiation between insight and analysis is something we are generally aware of in daily life. For example, we hear ourselves and others say, "don't overthink that too much" and "give it a while, it will come to you."

---

[31] Again see: *Remote brainwaves predict future 'Eureka' moment*, in Science Daily, September 12, 2018.

Again note, we do not have access to the precise details, the specific molecular and even electrical mechanisms of each form of insight function or AHA. We do not have a seat on the mini-micro level where the brain is electing the AHA insight pathway. What very specific mini-micro level switch (or stream) and or other decision function causes the brain to elect (or stumble into?) the AHA mode?

Is there something about this function we can trigger at will once we know how this works? How valuable it will be for us to be able to replicate the AHA function ever more at will. Imagine what a *conscious initiation of a conscious AHA, and then a conscious gestalt-like learning, a transfer learning for sustaining the AHA,* can mean in psychotherapy and related work with clients addressing problem addictions.

PRECURSORS TO THE AHA

Among the range of related research findings that have emerged are those addressing what may be precursors to insight AHAs such as positive mood[32] which "appears to broaden attention." On the other hand, "anxiety appears to narrow attention," at times quite necessarily such as in event of a person needing to focus on responding to a specific danger (e.g., escaping a predator).

***However, I do want to note here that the skilled clinician, psychotherapist, can identify and guide the energy, even if anxiety, trapped in a double bind to empower an effective release from this bind. In this sense, anxiety when adeptly navigated can be a path to a releasing AHA. (See Chapters 17, 18, 19, 24, 25.)

---

[32] John Kounios and Mark Berman, *The cognitive neuroscience of insight.* Annu. Rev. Psychol. 2014. 65:71–93

Another area of insight generating may be the effect of attention itself. Attentional control theory [33] suggests that anxiety moves through the brain in a bottom up (externally triggered) attention pattern where instinct and immediate survival-like mental modes are in play. With the reduction of anxiety, the top down (internally triggered) attentional mode is more likely to dominate.

Note that for purposes of the transformative learning involved in *Gestalting Addiction Processes*, it is in the top down mode that the brain has the opportunity to move into transformative processing and *AHA gestalting.*

****Continuing my above note, the skilled clinician, psychotherapist, can lead the client's attention from bottom up into top down processing modes that can generate the AHA release noted above.* (See *Part Six* for more on this process.)

So, both bottom up and top down attentional modes can at some point *trigger* their respective forms of: (a) bottom up *impulse driven* responsiveness, [34] and (b) top down *processing driven* problem solving, and also *insight driven* problem solving AHA realization.

PROBLEM ADDICTION

---

[33] Fumi Katsuki, et. al., *Bottom-up and top-down attention: different processes and overlapping neural systems.* PubMed Review Article, Dec. 20, 2013. <<https://doi.org/10.1177/1073858413514136>>

[34] "The individual's cognitive recognition of these negative consequences may lead to attempts to develop changed attitudes and [changed] drug-using behaviors. This process necessitates executive control [the brain's top-down executive control function] which may be mediated by top-down control of the prefrontal cortex over subcortical [and bottom-up] processes [that had been] promoting motivations to engage in the addictive behavior." [Mark Potenza, et. al., *Neuroscience of behavioral and pharmacological treatments for addictions.* Neuron. 2011. 2/24; 69(4):695-712.]

CAN ALSO TRIGGER
BOTTOM UP IMPULSE DRIVEN MODE

Clearly, the externally driven (bottom up, impulse) mode of processing, quite rightly narrows the focus to key and valid, even essential, triggers such as signs of actual external dangers and related urgencies/emergencies.

On the other hand, I have seen that *something else can also activate the bottom up mode,* something less life saving, such as infected, erroneously perceived, false dangers or shortages including seeming threats to *problem addiction's sense of stability,* e.g., withdrawal symptoms, cravings, and other sensations native to problem addiction patterns. Here, what I have earlier defined as the *relapse reflex* can be triggered.

Such seeming threats can be presented by the **problem addiction pattern programming's** *control of our attention and perception processes, even of our gestalts, our form completions.*
AHA AS A TOP DOWN BRAIN FUNCTION

On the opposite end of the attentional spectrum, top down, internally driven processing allows for sensations, information, and more subtle data generally in the mind's background, to engage, and even at times surface into, the consciousness. (Refer to the *Going Conscious Process* I describe in chapters of *Part Six.*)

Clearly, this top down, *internally triggered, AHA* is on the other end of the spectrum, opposite the bottom up *urgent impulse driven response* end of the spectrum. The top down AHA is virtually the polar opposite of the externally triggered bottom up fight-flight-freeze impulse response to actual danger, threats, shortages. And again, where there is a drug addiction for example, the bottom up impulse driven response can be triggered in the craving-relapse-use reflex cycle/pattern (which when responding to problem addiction's triggers and cues, is the infected gestalt at work). (See diagram at the end of this chapter.)

YET,
WE MUST SEE THIS***

Conscious discernment in AHA recognition is therefore essential. In my work with thousands of persons addressing problem addictions, I have seen the power and risks of what may appear to be AHAs (when they may actually be problem addiction driven impulses disguised as AHAs[35]).

Certainly, the AHA is powerful and tremendously useful. Yet, I again emphasize that some powerful mental experiences seem to be (*are programmed to disguise themselves as being*) AHAs and are not. Consider problem addiction's response to an intense craving, for example when the response is to rapidly find and use the drug being craved at all costs (the drug or other object/behavior of the problem addiction). Research has even documented this tendency, this *dirty needle now versus clean needle later immediate gratification impulse.*[36]

And there is so much more to learn regarding even insight itself: what authentic and healthy insight is, what generates it, what sustains (elevates) it; whether we can generate or encourage more and greater pivotal, even life changing, insight in ourselves, in our work, in our clients, in their recovery processes.

---

[35] As I note throughout this book, the problem addiction pattern seeks to preserve itself and even **dominate its host**—us—by moving into, invading, the normally functional patterning of normally healthy behaviors, decisions, cognitions, emotions.

[36] Refer to the *Psychobiological Profiles* volume of the *INTERNATIONAL COLLECTION ON ADDICTION* as noted in the recommended reading at the end of this present book, *GESTALTING ADDICTION*.

There is, however, also a great deal to determine regarding what may appear to be insight, a flash or rush of understanding or realizing, when it is not: when the AHA is what I describe as an **infected gestalt**, infected by the **invasive problem addiction program.*****

Is this an infected AHA?

EVER MORE
CONSCIOUS ACCESS AND CONTROL

If we can gain ever more conscious awareness of our brain's shift into AHA mode, might we have more valuable AHAs on a daily or at least weekly basis? Might we be able to discern the difference between a clear (and unaffected by invasive problem addiction) gestalt AHA, and one that is infected? ... Once we have more conscious access to our gestalt AHA processes, might we have more control over our own logical, emotional, and instinctual problem solving functions and insights?

Were we to gain such control over our AHA option, we might be able to make inroads into ourselves in new ways. And, this brings me back to my comments regarding the importance of the gestalt therapist (and or other psychotherapist) being highly trained and ready to truly and effectively guide the lead in to, the experience of, and the response to, the client's AHAs, paradoxical double binds, and other stages. (See *Parts Five* and *Six* where I suggest the role of the highly trained gestalt or other clinician as being designed to *orchestrate* the client's **AHA progression** into and through the recognizing and then sustaining of any positive effects of AHAs. See also *Part Six* for how I apply what I explain to my clients is the *juxtaposition in double bind release work for generating AHAs*.)

ESPECIALLY IN
THE CASE OF ADDICTION

Especially in the case of problem addiction, the AHA moment can be guided to help the client see, feel, know, the trap, no way out, no solution, closed loop, nature of problem addiction. The client can come face to face with the addiction programming that is…

designed to
preserve the addiction
over the person who is addicted.

The clinician/psychotherapist must be on alert for any rising, emerging, gestalt awarenesses, and also for any infection (such as by addiction programming itself) of any seeming gestalt AHAs that are actually *addiction driven impulses* disguised as AHAs. Clients can be guided in seeing this for themselves in the **Gestalting Addiction Processes** I introduce in *Part Six*.

TWO OF THE BRAIN'S NUMEROUS
PROBLEM SOLVING SCENARIOS

from "bottom of brain" up   ← ← → →   *from "top of brain" down*
externally triggered   **internally triggered**
response to danger/problem: **response to problem:**
FIGHT-FLIGHT-FREEZE   **AHA RESPONSE**
IMPULSE RESPONSE   (form, awareness completion)
within 200-500 milliseconds   *after 8 seconds*

↑

QUESTION:

DOES LOGICAL ANALYTICAL PROCESSING
FALL BETWEEN THE ENDS OF THE ABOVE SPECTRUM
OR ON ANOTHER ENTIRELY SEPARATE CONTINUUM?

not analytical

↑

mildly analytical

↑

highly analytical

5
Toward Higher Levels of Knowing: Gestalt Learning

Following an illness at the age of two, educator and activist for the disabled, Helen Keller, was blind and deaf. Her life story is that of a profound journey into strength and hope, and *learning*—learning and learning communication itself. Keller later told us, "Life is either a daring adventure or nothing."

POWER OF LEARNING

The power of learning can be brought into challenges, seemingly even "hopeless" situations, and open doors to otherwise not only closed but hitherto invisible avenues. Where we can, encouraging and guiding this desire to learn, this determination, and even *transformative life changing learning* itself, can help change the lives both of those teaching and of those learning.

Can the power of learning be brought to other challenges such as problem addiction? Now, some tell me at this point in my presentation of this material, that prayer is a more powerful change agent than learning, that "the heart is where change happens, not the head." I can agree, in general. However, the form of *learning that engages the whole person on all levels*, heart, mind, and soul, can be immensely powerful, life changing.

LEARNING TO MOVE OUT OF PARADOX

Let's pause a moment here and feel the lose-lose no-way-out distress-distress angst of problem addiction itself. There are few words that can portray in full the physically and emotionally draining, heart wrenching, even at times terrifying, anguish addiction can bring. Those who know the ragged path addiction drags some through report their angst most clearly:

"I've overdosed three times, and tried to commit suicide twice. But all this is trying to commit suicide, isn't it? It's like this addiction has a personality, has taken me over, and wants to kill me."

"I've spent the past ten years in and out of addiction treatment programs, and on and off of all kinds of medically assisted treatment that hasn't really helped me. Now I'm addicted to that stuff too, in addition to my own drugs and drinking. Nothing seems to work for me. I get moments or days or weeks or months of hope, then right back into the cycle. Even when I'm not using and drinking, I ride the roller coaster ride, a bit of hope and then crashing down into huge despair. I feel so stuck, trapped."

"I just don't see any way to change. I've done it all, I go to meetings, I take classes, I follow directions, and I pray, pray, and pray. But that nagging addiction feeling, it keeps sucking me in, like a black hole. My addiction keeps coming back, like a ghost waiting to sneak in again. I see other people doing what I do and doing so much better with their recoveries. I just can't seem to get it right. I'm losing hope, I am. Is there any way for me to finally get it?"

This kind of addiction pattern programming can lead to these distinct and all too common forms of human suffering. For these persons quoted above, and for so many others, addiction is a two edged sword, a lose-lose no-exit condition, a deadly paradox. With the high comes the low. With the pleasure comes the pain. With the addiction comes the problem of stopping the addiction, and life caught in what feels to be the never ending trapping cycle of addiction. Sure, there can be moments of hope, even AHAs. In these brief AHA times, a way out is glimpsed, and for a moment or a while hope steps forward.

What does it take to preserve this hope? What is it that we can *learn to shift us* **into a stage of our lives where hope takes hold, where what we learn works for us?**

Now, as noted in the previous chapter, we can look to the AHA experience. We can even seek this. (And as psychotherapists, we can seek to generate the AHA, as discussed in the chapters of *Part Six* of this book.) With the AHA we are (at least momentarily) released from a no-answer, no-solution, no-way-out *paradoxical double bind*. We are (at least temporarily) able to be released from all or part of a "stuck" (emotional and or cognitive) situation or condition, glimpsing a way out of what appears to be a blocked-blocked, lose-lose, nowhere to turn dilemma, a double binding no-exit trap such as problem addiction. (Refer to *Chapters 17, 18, 19*.)

How wonderful it is when we can make a great insight, an AHA, last. *When we can sustain the advance in awareness of the glimpse, of the insight AHA, we have elevated our awareness, in an elevation AHA, a gestalt learning. Now learning has taken place and been sustained.*

In work with clients who seek release from their own anguishes, their own double binds such as those of problem addiction, guided gestalt with transformative learning can sustain insights into elevations in awareness.

The sustaining I speak of here, to be most effective, powerful, ideally takes place on all levels, heart, mind, and soul, engaging as much of the SELF as we can. ACCESSING THE TRUE AND WHOLE SELF: this is where lasting personal change can actually take place.

SHIFTING TO A
HIGHER LEVEL OF KNOWING

The previous chapter noted the neural fireworks taking place in the brain during the eight seconds leading to the AHA. Following this AHA, for this AHA awareness to stay with us, to elevate us, we require a learning from this AHA, a sort of higher level transfer learning, a *gestalt learning*. Being aware of not only the AHA process, but of the *elevation* of the AHA via the gestalt learning process, is where we can build significant behavioral change.

This is where we can gain the power to overcome the problem addiction programming that has overtaken even our ability to think clearly, to know what is really happening to us – to even know that this invasive programming is there.

So many people caught in the wrenching struggle of drug/alcohol and other potentially destructive and potentially life threatening addictions (addictions to drugs/alcohol, or to behaviors such as gambling, gaming, spending, or dangerous sexual and or "love" relationships, etc.) face repeating hardship, endure ongoing relapses, repeatedly crashing and burning.

TRAPPED?

Like hamsters in cages, running round and round in their circular no exit cycles, or like ants following each other as they spiral down into their no exit death traps…

Humans suffering in their problem addiction patterns are being directed by insidious addiction programming to go on and on and on, to remain trapped in the problem addiction patterns, even in the face of harm to themselves or others as a result. For too many, the addiction programming directs them to stay trapped in the problem cycle/pattern until they die from these very addictions

that drive them, have programmed them, to die of their addictions.

The trapping of the individual's energy and will in the addiction double bind is the addiction pattern's hold on its host's energy and will. However, the energy held, stuck, in this trap can be carefully guided and released to *catalyze personal transformation*.

UNLOCKING THE AHA

Can an insight, an AHA, really make any difference? Yes, if guided to its full potential. In the **AHA** *release* from a double binding[37] wrong-wrong, don't know-don't know, no-relief no-relief state (state of not seeing enough to *correctly* complete the exit or solution picture, not "seeing" what we need to know to do so), we are *shifting to a higher level of "seeing."* We are *shifting to another knowing (another level of learning).*

This *shift* is key in both cognitive and emotional (many are cognitive-emotional combined) AHA events and therefore can be highly relevant in psychotherapy processes aimed at personal shifts. (Certainly, addiction treatment and addiction focused

---

[37] The early Double Bind Theory, originally offered by Gregory Bateson and his team mid 20th century, defines the double bind as a "communication dilemma" arising when one is receiving two or more messages that conflict. This renders a wrong-wrong situation in that any use of one of these conflicting messages will be read as wrong by the opposing or conflicting message/s. We can see this when two parents of the same child give that child opposite (or what sound to be opposite) responses, directions, or rules. We can also see this when even just one parent gives her or his child conflicting directions or messages such as "do it this way," then "no, do it that other way," and then back and forth as if no way is the right way.

therapy seek to promote personal "shifts" with behavior change implications.)

Let's briefly unpack this notion that learning and even behavior change can be brought about (or as I like to describe this, *catalyzed*) by higher ("deutero" and beyond) levels of learning, and see how the double bind concept is so very relevant here.

EMPOWERING
THE SHIFT
TO ANOTHER
LEVEL OF AWARENESS

Let's start by unpacking the shift present in moving to a higher level of knowing. First, let's back up and think of the insight AHA. This insight AHA is in essence a glimpse of another level of knowing, awareness, consciousness. We have the experience of seeing there is more to know. This seeing there is MORE TO KNOW is the insight AHA itself, a view of another level of knowing.

As noted by Albert Einstein: "No problem can be solved from the same level of consciousness that created it." Gregory Bateson, addressing his own Theory of Learning, also discussed this matter of seeing or knowing from a broader or higher perspective. Bateson taught that:

**We cannot see the problem
from within the level of the awareness
of the problem.**

**We must be able to move, shift, to a
new level of awareness, of learning, to see.**

Once we realize there is more to know, we can move to make this shift, to know this *more there is to know*. We can learn to sustain this insight. In the *gestalting of addiction* I am introducing herein (see *Part Six*), sustaining the *gestalt insight* (as in *Chapter 4*) involves *gestalt learning* (as in *Chapter 5*).

THEORIES OF LEARNING
IN ADDICTION

General learning theory tells us that even addiction is a learned behavior. The basic understanding is that learning takes one or all of at least three forms:

(a) *Classical conditioning* learns to *link* or *pair* an experience with something we relate to that experience, such as a sensation with a cue. For example, in addiction we may link the pleasure or "high" of engaging in the addiction behavior with cues, triggers, events we grow to associate as regular elements of the "high" experience.

(b) *Operant conditioning* learns to link an action with its consequences or reinforcement. For example, in addiction, we may learn to link the use of a drug with the rewarding, positively reinforcing, "high" associated with that use. In operant conditioning we associate the consequence with the behavioral choice.

(c) *Social learning* learns by watching others. This is learning by observation. When we are close to or related to those we are observing and learn by observing them, we may do what I describe as *learning by identity.*

In the addiction and other behavioral fields, the general view is that when something such as an addiction related behavior has been learned, it can be *unlearned*. This *counter conditioning* involves either: (a) providing a distinctly negative experience as a result of an action such as use of a drug to which we are addicted; or, (b) repeating an alternative behavior so frequently it is learned and ideally overrides the problem behavior programming.

LEVELS OF TRANSFORMATIONAL LEARNING

Bateson's Theory of Learning introduced a framework for levels of learning, and for possibilities of *transformational learning.* Bateson embraced the notion that each higher level system is built from systems on lower levels. (Each higher or bigger picture or understanding is built upon smaller parts or lower levels of the whole picture or understanding. And yes, of course, the higher level understanding is more than simply the sum of smaller understandings: the whole "understanding" or learning is greater than the sum of its parts.)

Of note is the first on Bateson's listed criteria of mind: "A mind is an aggregate of interacting parts or components." This aggregate is the larger picture, the whole. Note that Bateson refers to the mind being an *aggregate* of components of the mind. Bateson does not view this aggregation, or any sudden realization that may at times occur within this aggregation, as magical per se.

Rather, a realization, a shift, constitutes a *constructive change in awareness,* one that is built on communication among levels of mental processes such as *levels of learning.* (When we consider Bateson's Levels of Learning as I detail below, the second level or deutero learning he refers to does include a gestalt sort of shift in awareness or understanding.)

GESTALT LEARNING

Bateson highlighted the notion that there are levels of learning, each level either not advancing (Learning Level 0) or actually advancing the transfer of prior learning yet only to the same reoccurring situation (Learning Level 1). Or the learning can be more profound, more an actual transfer. The transfer can be to different context(s) based on the realization and connecting of relevant prior learning (Learning Level 2).

Here I simplify these levels of learning in the interest of brevity and do encourage Readers to directly review Bateson's material, as there is so much more in his direct words than I can address in this brief book.[38] Note that I add in to these definitions of learning levels my comments about the AHA insight, and transferring, sustaining, the learning or AHA. (See *Chapters 17, 18, 19* for more on this matter.)

Learning Level 0:
Touch a hot iron and get burned. Pull your hand away.
Then touch the same hot iron again and get burned again.
No learning about touching the hot iron has taken place.
No apparent learning at this Learning Level 0.

Learning Level 1:
Touch a hot iron and get burned.
Then do not touch the same or another hot iron –
as you have learned touching any hot iron can burn you.
Here the learning has been **transferred** *from being*
about the first hot iron to being about any hot iron.
Learned not to touch any hot iron at this Learning Level 1.

Learning Level 2:
Touch a hot iron and get burned.
Then do not touch a hot iron again, or any other very hot metal,
as these can burn you.
And do avoid other self harm as self harm hurts.***
Here the learning has **transferred** *from learning that touching a hot iron can burn, to learning that touching other hot metal can also*

---

[38] See Gregory Bateson's seminal 1972 book, *STEPS TO AN ECOLOGY OF MIND.*

burn/harm, to also transfer learning that harm hurts, to then also transfer learning to know to avoid self harm as self harm hurts.

Applying or **transferring** what has been learned about a hot iron to other hot metal, and to self harm, is the second level or gestalt "deutero learning" of *Learning Level 2*.

<u>*Learned, at this Learning Level 2, not to touch hot metal, and that harm hurts, so to avoid self harm. This is a* **learning to learn**.</u>[39]

<u>*Learning Level 3:*</u>

The learning to avoid self harm noted above***

in *Learning Level 2* can also be said to be *Learning Level 3*.

As this AVOID SELF HARM learning develops on,

it can transfer rather broadly.

It is said that fewer people experience *Learning Level 3* and beyond, which would be an even higher level of learning transfer. (I tend to believe this is not quite the case, and that this level of learning can be experienced and taught.) When the transfer of the learning is a still more profound and lasting **leap** in understanding, in awareness, then *Learning Level 3* and beyond has taken place.

<u>*Learning/realizing more about being burned, even about being harmed in other ways, and about self harm itself -- and even what to do to avoid this harm can be Learning Level 3 and beyond.*</u>

DUETERO AND BEYOND LEARNING
AS

---

[39] One of my earlier books, *LEARNING TO LEARN*, and my earlier works on **metacognition** conducted in that same time period, are in essence all about *thinking about thinking* and *being aware of one's awareness*, of one's thought processes. For more on *being aware of awareness*, see *UNVEILING THE HIDDEN INSTINCT*, and *THE GOING CONSCIOUS PROCESS*, as well as *KEYS TO PERSONAL DISCOVERY*. See reading list at the end of this present book, *GESTALTING ADDICTION*.

GESTALT LEARNING

We can get trapped in behavioral, emotional, spiritual, and cognitive double binds, messes, morasses such as miserable, seemingly no exit problem addiction patterns. And this is exactly where these patterns are programmed to hold us: trapped in these patterns.

Fortunately, this is also where a great deal of energy is stored, blocked, locked in. This is where the release of trapped energy can yield transformative, lasting, gestalt learning that can shift us, raise us, to a new level of understanding, awareness, emotion, and behavior. The key in gestalt learning is the release from the double bind of not having a solution, of not knowing a way out of a problem (such as a seeming no exit problem addiction pattern).

Recognizing and utilizing the double binds we get caught in, trapped in, and understanding the *power of release from these binds*, can mobilize lasting personal change. (See Chapters of *Part Six*, especially *Chapters 17, 18* and *19*, where I delve into the *paradoxical double bind*, the energy locked in such a bind, and its release.

Gregory Bateson taught a great deal about what he called the double bind,[40] which he had introduced to others much earlier (as

---

[40] In the 1950s, several researchers attributed schizophrenia to dysfunctional communications in the family. Bateson proposed his original theory of the double bind which said that contradictions in family communications predisposes its members to schizophrenia. [Mathijis Keepmans, *Schizophrenia and the family: double bind theory revisited*. International Congress of Psychology, Montreal, Canada. August 1996.]
Although this theory of schizophrenia has been discarded, **the double bind itself lives on as a concept and reality in numerous arenas such as in Bateson's application of the double bind in addiction (alcoholism).** Bateson

far back as the 1950s), and also about the AHA-like release from the double bind. I am grateful for the insights Bateson offered, and note that I as many others have continued over time to be affected by and apply elements of Bateson's thinking in our various careers and work.

What struck many of us was (and still is) the notion of the double bind as it applied (and still applies) to a range of critical situations. In essence, the double bind is the cognitive and emotional trap, locked in sense, that accompanies the dilemma that arises when one is receiving two or more conflicting messages. For example, the child is told, "Go get your blue coat" and does so, only to then hear, "No, I said get your red coat, do that now," and complies, only to then hear, "No, the blue coat is better, go put that on," and the child complies, only to hear this was not right, and so on, with no correct behavior. The confusion, suffering, emotional turmoil, even psychological disorders that can result from ongoing wrong-wrong lose-lose communication being received (especially during childhood), is marked and can be quite serious.

THE DOUBLE BINDING
NATURE OF ADDICTION ITSELF

Let's look more closely at this paradox, this double bind, this no exit trap. It is my view that problem addiction is its own multi-level

---

wrote, "If double binds cause anguish and despair... then it follows, conversely, that for healing these wounds ... some converse of [release from] the double bind will be appropriate. [Release from the] double bind leads to the conclusion of [the] despair, [release from the sense that] 'There are no alternatives.' [Here] the *Serenity Prayer* explicitly frees the worshipper from these maddening bonds." [See Gregory Bateson, *The cybernetics of 'self': a theory of alcoholism*. Oceanic Institute Hawaii. Pages 1-18.]

double bind closing in on itself, a bind within a bind within a bind. (See *Chapters 18, 25,* and *26.*)

To give in to the craving (which is key in the problem addiction pattern), which in substance addiction can be to relapse, to use the drug again, is to experience one of the lose experiences in the basic lose-lose scenario. The opposing, conflicting, lose experience can be the experience of not using the drug and "suffering" through the craving, even withdrawal, again.

Problem addiction is where the rubber meets the road, at least in double bind terms. Addiction is a programming to repeat-cycle, over and over and over and over again. There is no way out, or no easy way out, once the problem addiction sets in. The cycle perpetuates itself rather predictably. The triggers (or as I call these, the *tertiary and secondary* triggers--and then if needed by the problem pattern for pressing the host--*us*--further into the addiction pattern cycle, the *primary* triggers) are experienced. The response to a trigger may be in increments, steps in drift (such as "relapse drift") or craving or urge toward partaking in the addiction behavior yet again. Or relapse may be an immediate impulse driven response to cravings, triggers, etc. Either way, the trigger-urge-response cycle is perpetuated by the problem addiction program. (See the cycle pattern diagram at the end of this chapter.)

The effort to stop using the drug (again, alcohol is also a drug) or engaging in the "so-called non-drug" behavior (such as gambling) to which one is addicted is frequently met with a strong emotional and physical desire, craving, longing, not to stop using or doing the addicted and addictive behavior. The cycle is already in place and is re-triggered, reactivated, rather rapidly. From there on, use and experience the brief high and then the effects of using. Or don't use and experience the longing, the craving to use. Hence a lose-lose no-exit seeming double bind.

LEARNING AND
BEHAVIOR CHANGE

Although somewhat unaware of the double bind concept, much of addiction therapy and addiction treatment nevertheless seeks to promote healthy changes in behavior. Ideally, further understanding the **energy locked in a double bind addiction pattern** can empower addiction treatment and addiction therapy.

Learning is central in this work. Thus, the linking of the emotional with the cognitive processes is being done in a range of treatment and therapy contexts. Without delving into the specific nature of several of these approaches, [41] I do want to note here, even to highlight and emphasize here, that the gestalting of deeply embedded truths, the *catalytic nature of actual gestalting*, is rarely specifically and professionally addressed, let alone promoted to its maximum positive potential—in large part as a result of lack of available information and limited options for authentic and highly informed professional training in this area, and also due to misunderstandings regarding the potent nature of what I describe as the **true activated gestalt (TAG)**. [Note, I say "TRUE ACTIVATED GESTALT (TAG)" here to differentiate even from the various versions of what is called "new" gestalt.]

WE MAY NOT NOTICE
SOME OF OUR
LEARNINGS

---

[41] Examples include CBT, Cognitive Behavioral Therapy, and DBT, Dialectical Behavioral Therapy. These methods were preceded by Ralph Ellis' REBT, Rational Emotive Behavioral Therapy. Ellis has been considered the "father of cognitive therapy."

Frequently in life, we are presented (or present ourselves) with a range of situations—issues, challenges, even problem addictions—all requiring some degree of our attention. Some of these situations we resolve without even realizing we have been addressing these as so much work is done on our sub- and even un- conscious levels.

Indeed, quite often we are backburner-ing or stuffing away an issue or situation so as to focus on other matters, yet we are addressing what we are stuffing away somehow, somewhere in our minds. And then, suddenly, the issue or situation demands our attention, calls us, pulls on us. Or then, suddenly we realize we have not solved a problem and now it is front and center on our minds.

Problem solving is part of life. So is the process of seeking to overcome problem patterns, although we are not always consciously aware we are so doing. After all, we tell ourselves, the living organism wants to survive, not to fall prey to threats to its well being, even to its existence (*such as problem drug and non-drug addictions*).

TRANSFORMATIVE LEARNING CAN MAKE THE DIFFERENCE

So the living organism is naturally drawn to maintain healthy patterns, healthy addictions, not problem patterns, problem addictions. Thus, the living organism is drawn to develop an exit or new response as a way out of a problem pattern (the problem addiction pattern). This *NEW RESPONSE* is indicated in the *NEW RESPONSE - PATTERN EXIT OPTION** at the bottom of the diagram at the end of this chapter. Although a simple asterisk* marks the *NEW RESPONSE - PATTERN EXIT OPTION** in the diagram, this *EXIT* is no minor cognitive, emotional, spiritual, and behavioral shift. Here an *insight AHA* has taken place: a *way out of the trap*, the double binding no exit addiction cycle, has been glimpsed. *Now there is the opportunity to SUSTAIN this NEW RESPONSE* by elevating this AHA via transformative gestalt learning.*

Without understanding what **transformative learning** is, we may miss the opportunity to change our lives, even following an AHA. Indeed, in an almost counter survival manner, we all too often find ourselves feeling trapped in paradoxical double binding problem addiction patterns that continue to pull us back into and trap us in their cycles (such as the trigger-urge-use pattern diagramed at the end of this chapter).

The *pull* imposed upon us by the problem addiction programming is the drive, the lure, the pressure, the perceived need, to remain trapped in the problem addiction cycle pattern. This is what the problem addiction pattern program exists to do, to trap its hosts—us—in difficult to break cycles/patterns of addiction. So the addiction program pulls us to remain under its control.

Overriding this pull is the challenge. This breaking free requires release of the energy (your energy, our energy) the problem cycle pattern works to keep trapped in its no exit double bind.

PROBLEM/CHALLENGE:
TO LEAVE THE PROBLEM PATTERN (CYLCE),
TO DEVELOP AND ENGAGE IN A

NEW RESPONSE*

PROBLEM PATTERN

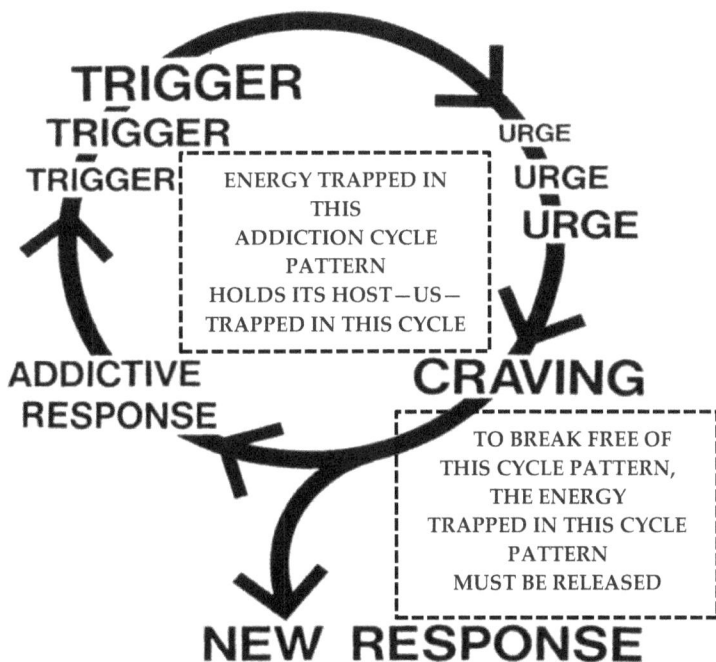

TRIGGER
TRIGGER
TRIGGER

URGE
URGE
URGE

ENERGY TRAPPED IN THIS
ADDICTION CYCLE PATTERN
HOLDS ITS HOST — US —
TRAPPED IN THIS CYCLE

ADDICTIVE
RESPONSE

CRAVING

TO BREAK FREE OF
THIS CYCLE PATTERN,
THE ENERGY
TRAPPED IN THIS CYCLE PATTERN
MUST BE RELEASED

NEW RESPONSE

PATTERN EXIT OPTION*

RELEASED ENERGY PROPELS TEMPORARY EXIT
FROM THIS ADDICTION CYCLE PATTERN,
A RELEASE THAT CAN BE SUSTAINED TO STAY
FREE OF THIS CYCLE

6
Clarifying,
Revising,
And Reviving
Gestalt On A New Platform:
Gestalting Addiction Itself

Various views of all the old and new gestalt material—its theory, psychology, learning, therapy, and offshoots—have emerged. I find that it is the bridging of these various fields of gestalt that empowers gestalt work, gestalt therapy, the gestalt experience. This can bring together the concepts of: gestalt perception (especially the form completion I emphasize herein), the gestalt AHA, gestalt learning, various gestalt therapy techniques, etc., to set the stage for the *Gestalting Addiction Processes* I introduce in this book.

As I noted in *Chapter 2*, the *Overview* of this book, one of the greatest criticisms of gestalt is that the original gestalt theory of the early 20th century assumed that perceptual gestalt processes were set, innate.[42] As per my comments in *Chapter 2*, both research and societal views have moved past the restriction of perception to the biological realm. In our "modern" times, we have come to see what a powerful and determining influence environment has on the individual, including on the individual's perception, cognition,

---

[42] See review of gestalt psychology and gestalt theory in Johan Wagemans, et. al., *A century of gestalt psychology in visual perception.* Psychological Bulletin, 2012 Nov:138(6):1172-1217.

learning, emotion, action—including on his or her problem addiction behaviors.

CLARIFYING, REVIVING, AND REVISING GESTALT

However justified the assault on old (biologically based) gestalt theory has been, there has been little reason to throw the entire baby out with the bath water. I say that there are, among gestalt theory, gestalt psychology, gestalt learning, gestalt in therapy, and gestalt therapy itself, some powerful understandings that can be further developed and brought forward in a new light.

To wit, the **gestalting of addiction** I propose in this book brings together, clarifies, distills, and then rethinks, adapts, and moves forward:

(a) Gestalt theory, gestalt psychology, gestalt learning, and other gestalt-like concepts of perception and learning where these can be joined and synergistically applied to guiding behavior change;

(b) The notion of *the* gestalt, bridging the concepts of the *gestalted* insight, the gestalt AHA, and further rethinkings of the gestalt AHA event/moment itself, to empower their use in behavior change therapy.

I do so to add new perspectives and dimensions to:

(c) The application of gestalt, its theories, definitions, and concepts;

(d) What I call gestalt *work*, some of which has called or currently calls itself gestalt therapy;

(e) Gestalt (and related) work in behavior change processes such as those involved in addressing problem addictions; and,

(f)   The notion (I develop herein) of having ourselves, others, and even addiction itself reveal and gestalt itself (ourselves, themselves, itself) and its (our, their, its) true nature.

PRECIOUS AND POWERFUL GESTALTS

As I explain in *Parts Five* and *Six* of this book, I have found there to be great room for further development and clarification of understandings, definitions, and applications of gestalt. I have found there are **precious gestalts** (for example, AHAs, identifications, and releases) **of buried emotions, patterns, and conditions that can be carefully guided and cultivated** by expert and highly ethical professionals who have been carefully trained in the application of gestalt techniques and tools—and who understand and respect the consequences of such work.

Clients frequently seek this sort of therapy, although they tend not to have precise labels and definitions for it. Some of these people arrive in my office talking about newly surfacing (and or resurfacing) challenging emotional responses to earlier—years earlier—gestalt or other therapy experiences (as noted in *Chapter 3*). Some say that now the impacts of those experiences are registering markedly, at times uncomfortably.

What has gone on in there, within these persons' psyches? What have they carried since those earlier gestalt (and or other forms of) therapy experiences? We cannot go to that precise moment in that earlier time, nor wade through neural recordings of interpretations of these earlier experiences. We can serve these clients by working with them regarding what they are currently presenting as their experiences.

SEEKING THE
PIVOTAL AHA
IN ADDICTION THERAPY

The highly aware clinician can see, sense, feel, the moment when the *client first comes face to face with the problem addiction that has moved into (invaded, even perhaps subsumed) much of the natural programming, the basic neural wiring, of this client.* Here is where guidance can allow this client to meet her or his addiction, to come face to face with the conceptual, virtual space between the addiction program and the self. (In this process, conceiving of a boundary between the self and the problem addiction program afflicting the self can be a useful visualization type exercise.) (See *Chapters 24, 25, 26.*)

This may sound simple. However, it is *careful, highly informed and sensitive, psychotherapeutic guiding* that can help the client navigate this process, see more and more each time "inside" her or him SELF. This is how the client can see that she or he is NOT the problem addiction, despite the problem addiction's invasion of (infiltration into) that client's mind and even identity.

PROBLEM/CHALLENGE:
DIFFERENTIATING THE SELF
FROM THE PROBLEM PATTERN

THE PROBLEM PATTERN'S GOAL IS TO MERGE WITH
THE HOST, WITH THE PERSON, TO FULLY INSTATE
ITSELF AS THE DOMINANT PATTERN
WITHIN ITS HOST.
The trigger-urge-craving addicted response cycle (pattern)
below is NOT the host's pattern, it is the
invasive problem addiction program's pattern/cycle.

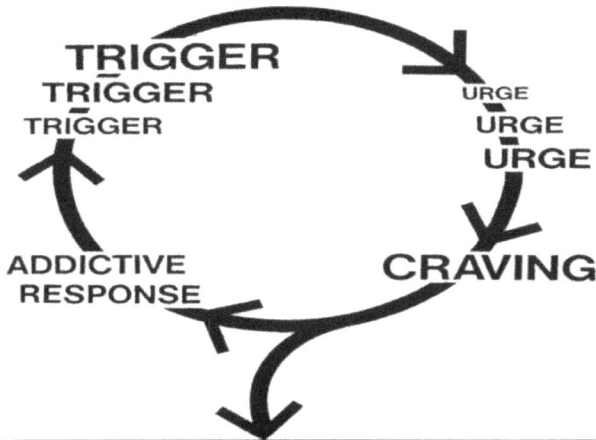

TRIGGER
TRIGGER
TRIGGER

URGE
URGE
URGE

CRAVING

ADDICTIVE
RESPONSE

TO STEP OUT OF THIS PROBLEM PATTERN,
THE HOST, THE PERSON, MUST
SEPARATE FROM THIS PROBLEM PATTERN.
THE HOST, THE SELF, MUST DIFFERENTIATE FROM
THE PROBLEM PATTERN:
THE SELF MUST FULLY KNOW AND LIVE THE
TRUTH
WHICH IS:
I, THE HOST, AM
NOT THIS PROBLEM PATTERN ADDICTION.

Part Three:

Faces of Gestalt

Face To Face
formed from artwork
by anonymous art therapy workshop participant

7
Toward Unveiling
The True Gestalt

It is time to rethink addiction as well as the role of (the) gestalt in addressing addiction. This rethinking is intensely simple, yet rather complex in its deviation from traditional approaches to addiction and the treatment of addiction, as well as to forms of psychotherapy, gestalt therapy, and other counseling provided persons seeking to address their addictions.

BACK TO GESTALT

In developing my perspective on addiction, I have again and again found myself back to the matter of gestalt (e.g., the many faces of gestalt learning, [43] gestalt psychology, gestalt theory, and the various forms of gestalt and other therapy). By gestalt here I refer to not just the therapy calling itself gestalt, but to the overarching macro (psycho-social and even political) and micro (neural, molecular, even synaptic) "brain" process(es) of gestalt.

I have come to see the profound linkage between core notions of gestalt, and the truth about addiction, especially the notions of: gestalt learning; the AHA; the understanding that the whole is greater than the sum of its parts; and the resulting understanding that we do not see (perceive, sense, feel, know) all there is to see

---

[43] The learning theory, with its deutero and gestalt learning, as set forth by Gregory Bateson, continues to influence my thinking regarding gestalt, addiction, cognition, perception, and behavior change.

(perceive, sense, feel, know). From these understandings, it is clear that we can form a further understanding of addiction itself. Indeed...

It is time for a shift in the way we
understand and address addiction.
It is time for the true gestalt of the true addiction.
In this, we will see so much about ourselves, our species,
and the challenges
we as individuals and as a species are facing.

We are indeed creatures of habit, wired with highly addict-able programming. Knowing this about ourselves can allow us to look more deeply at who we are (and are not). For example, as I explain in several ways in this book, we are *not* our addictions, we are *not* our programming to become addicted.

THE MATTER OF GESTALT

Although the label, "gestalt *therapy*," comes and goes from explicit use and popularity, I see its lingering and ongoing thematic and "strategic" influence. This influence continues to underly the development and application of so many psychotherapy and counseling techniques and perspectives. Meanwhile, the ongoing research on gestalt theory as per visual/perceptual processing functions persists in its great and highly valid significance.

Herein, I explain my thinking, which is that the ***gestalt itself*** **is still more far reaching than has thus far been understood**. THE gestalt is an event and a process, an insight and an action. In introducing the ***gestalting addiction*** I share in this book, I am calling for new understandings of both addiction and gestalt. In fact, I talk directly to addiction itself, calling upon ***addiction itself to gestalt itself***...

114

... to step forward with the truth about itself,
about what is really happening here,
about what and who this
invasive problem addiction programming
actually is,
as it is *not* us.

This addiction program invades us,
hides within us to use us,
and poses as us, disguises as us,
but it is *not* us.

MANY PSYCHOTHERAPIES

Influences and streams of gestalt theory and gestalt psychology are present in so many areas of clinical work. Clinicians and practitioners, (psychotherapists, counselors, and a range of others) are applying elements of gestalt therapy styles and approaches, frequently without naming these as stemming from gestalt, even at times without realizing they are so doing.

As the field(s) of addiction treatment have emerged and continued to develop myriad faces and forms, myriad "psychotherapies" and "approaches" have been and are being developed and applied. Psychotherapies and related processes have included but are not limited to: psychoanalysis, gestalt therapy, various behavior therapies such as the rational emotive and cognitive behavioral therapies, and other therapies among which are expressive therapy and narrative therapy. (While I discuss various forms of therapy in other publications, here I list these simply to generalize regarding psychotherapy.)

Also note that other more generally non-psychotherapy or somewhat psychotherapy-like approaches exist and are quite common in addiction treatment and addiction therapy. These have and do include but are not limited to intervention-type processes, some echoing what were already decades earlier called "tough-love" approaches. Tough love has in many ways been a valuable concept, as it addresses the tendency of those who love (or address) an addicted person to look away from the problem, to shy away from the truth about this addiction, to "go easy" on (perhaps even enable or co-depend upon) someone's addiction. The tough love approach directly confronts the addicted person to counter the tendency of both the addicted person and her/ his loved ones to look away or not address the addiction "head on."

Of note here is the winding of tough-love-like assertive approaches through so much of addiction treatment work. Over the years, assertive confrontation in treating addiction continues although rarely still calling itself tough love. [44] Streams of assertive approaches flow through much addiction treatment including some addiction focused gestalt therapy and other addiction related psychotherapy and counseling. (Known for his aggressive and confrontational style of gestalt therapy, the [for some questionable]

_____

[44] The "tough love" approach emerged in the 1980s as per a book by Phyllis and David York who had three daughters experiencing drug addiction. As parents they chose to draw the line, for example to refuse to allow a daughter to come home until she had gone into treatment for her addiction. In the years since, science has taught us more about the brain and addiction, showing that addiction is a chronic brain disease and many individuals with this disease cannot simply choose at will to stop using their drugs or drinking. Hence tough love is now viewed as a last resort approach. Although this is the case, I have seen elements of tough love surface in many current programs, although not being labelled as this tough love.

influence of Fritz Perls, one of the founders of gestalt therapy, can be said to still continue along these lines.[45])

ASSERTIVE CONFRONTATION

One of the primary pros of an assertive confrontation type approach to addiction is that many cases of addiction may be life threatening if not controlled and stopped. This life threat in essence lends an emergency measure to the work: i.e., in an emergency, few holds are barred to save a life. Assertion thus surfaces in the face of the implicit and at times even explicit urgency in much addiction treatment.

---

[45] Let us <u>not</u> assume all gestalt therapy takes on Fritz Perls' style. Note that Fritz Perls' gestalt therapy approach was known for its confrontational style. The later conjoining of tough love-like confrontation with therapy was a rather natural fit for some gestalt therapists modeling themselves after Fritz Perls. Perls himself was known for his theatrical and aggressive therapy style. **Additionally, according to some reports, Fritz Perls was also known for his sexist and aggressive treatment of women.** [See Jeffrey M. Masson, *Against Therapy: Emotional Tyranny and the Myth of Psychological Healing*. Common Courage Press, 1988.] **Jeffrey Masson writes that Perls was not only a sexist, but physically and emotionally abusive toward women in his private life.** Fritz Perls himself wrote in the original version, early edition, of his own book, *In and Out of the Garbage Pail*: "I got her down again and said, gasping: 'I've beaten up more than one bitch in my life.' Then she got up, threw her arms around me: 'Fritz, I love you.' Apparently she finally got what, all her life, she was asking for, and there are thousands of women like her in the States. Provoking and tantalizing, bitching, irritating their husbands and never getting their spanking. You don't have to be a Parisian prostitute to need that so as to respect your man." <u>Readers, please note</u>: *This sort of attitude is <u>not</u> common and <u>not</u> appreciated among most psychotherapists.*

Direct, even assertive, confrontation versus "softer" approaches have emerged within the earlier listed and other therapies and treatments for addiction. The general thinking driving assertive confrontation in treating addicted persons has been, and continues to be in many cases, that, "a forceful approach is the surest if not only method of reaching an addicted person, getting that person to hear and respond to treatment, to make getting clean and sober the highest priority."

THE
DENIAL WALL

I have seen so many treatment professionals and their clients and patients hit a wall of "no progress," of "not getting through," and at times beat their (metaphorical) heads against this wall. As I have watched this in hundreds of cases, I have seen, more like felt, the stand-off-like confrontation of energies: a "this is urgent, you must deal with this, you must hear me" treatment provider voice versus a "stop it, you are wrong, my problem isn't that bad; I don't need to or want to listen to you," or an "I can't understand what you are saying to me," or an "I just cannot do this, I just cannot quit using my drug/s" client/patient response.

DENIAL
IS THE WORD

Many treatment advocates and treatment professionals have seen this wall, this place of the "no" experienced and expressed by so many clients and patients. While the wall I speak of here takes various emotional and verbal, even social, forms, the commonality across all forms of this wall is that the wall can be sensed, felt, experienced, as its resistance is almost palpable.

Yes, there is an actual *feel* to this wall. The *denial* fortifying this wall is itself practically tangible. So called denial comes to life like an elephant in the room, one waiting to be recognized, hiding in plain sight, lurking and even dominating from the corners of the minds we are working with. I say that even when we feel we have helped our clients and patients "move past their denials of their addictions," we must watch for deeper levels of denial, ever more implicit and even hidden denials.

And more importantly, we must watch for this seeming denial presenting itself as, disguising itself as, denial, when it is not denial but rather a far more complex and insidious expression coming from not the client, but from the addiction pattern programming invading, occupying, that client.

DENIAL IS A MASK
THE PROBLEM ADDICTION PATTERN
WEARS
TO DISGUISE ITSELF
AS ITS HOST—AS US.

The basic notion of denial is presented in most all addiction therapies and treatments. The term, "denial," has become so popular that I hear it virtually everywhere in the addiction treatment world, almost recited as a given. As the delineation of what is often described as "the addict's denial" has become more and more pronounced, denial continues to be approached in addiction treatment and therapy as a given—as well as a major behavior, attitude, even force to be reckoned with, confronted, even aggressively confronted.

In so doing, *confrontation*, whether defining itself as tough love or a confrontational form of gestalt therapy, or any other of the many forms that confrontation finds its way into, streams through much of the work of treating addiction.

Confrontation is frequently viewed
as the most effective antidote to denial.
Yet, whose denial is this,
the client's
or the addiction programming's denial function?

WHERE
GESTALT THERAPY
HIT A NERVE

It was the latter part of the 20th century when, somewhere in the stream of approaches to addiction, addiction oriented gestalt therapy showed its face. Although gestalt therapy itself was a specialty not many knew in addiction treatment, the addiction treatment field was in essence receptive, as tough love-like thinking was tilling the ground and demonstrating that assertive confrontation could be a strong tool. Additionally, the tough and resistant nature of addiction itself appeared to be, according to some, "asking for confrontation."

Then, given both the (at times almost mandatory) self revealing and confrontational aspects that had come into some forms of gestalt therapy (i.e., Fritz Perls' work[46]), gestalt therapy, along with gestalt-like therapy, rather readily found a place in the addiction treatment world.

---

[46] Fritz Perls' work was central in the origination and development of gestalt therapy. Perls was indeed known for his keen observation skill, as well as for his dramatic, some even said "theatrical" and confrontational, even some described as "abrasive" gestalt therapy style. Perls did later speak out against his original presentation of gestalt, however he generally remained associated with his original abrasive aimed at cathartic style. Two streams of gestalt therapy were then emerging, one this Fritz Perls-like "cathartic" model, and the other a "dialogic paradoxical theory of change" model. [See Petruska Clarkson, Jennifer Mackewn, *Frits Perls (Key Figures in Counselling and Psychotherapy Series)*. 1993. P.6.]

At times, some psychotherapists explained that it was the "braver" therapist who dared to confront. In gestalt therapy circles, it was those adhering to a Fritz Perls' confrontational style who at times even bragged about their prowess in the more aggressive, confrontational style of therapy. At other times, it appeared to some observers that it was the possible lack of other clinical skills that left confrontation as a ready (or at times only) "tool."

I have watched forms of gestalt therapy surface in many addiction treatment approaches and programs, even when not labeling (or knowing) themselves as gestalt (or gestalt-like) therapy. In fact, both the confrontational aspects and the depth work taking place in much of gestalt therapy found their way into and were often (and still are) relabeled as something other than gestalt therapy, sometimes simply therapy or group therapy, or counseling group work.

YET THE GESTALT
STILL WAITS
TO BE DETECTED

Still, as I explain to my students, interns, and clients, THE gestalt itself is not therapy, it is a perceptual process, a form completion, a reality estimation, perhaps even a reality deception (in that the gestalt form completion never has the true and whole information to reveal the true whole of our reality).

It appears that the actual spirit, the full nature, the real energy and power of the gestalt itself, remains to be discovered.

Unveiling the true gestalt is the challenge now, both in addiction treatment and in the world around us. What deeply buried, disguised presences, can be revealed in a journey navigated by our inner gestalt gestalting itself, gestalting the journey itself? Who is in there, who will we find deep down? What awaits our discovery? Is what awaits hiding here in plain sight? Is it the invader, the addiction pattern program? How is it that we have been evolved or designed this way?

8
Faces of Gestalt

The road to realization can be formed with twists and turns, revelations and stunning insights. The journey itself can be central in the profound AHA to come. For me, gaining a deep understanding of the brain, and of the "addicted brain" (as science frequently calls it), led me to understanding what all this is really telling me.

It is as if the entire process of seeing and living the evolution of the "modern" addiction field has itself been a gestalt, at times a long drawn out one, at times one calling me to question just about everything I had been told by some of the self named "leaders" and "innovators" in various fields, including the fields of gestalt therapy and addiction treatment.

This journey has brought me to see addiction for what it is, for why it is treated the way it is, for how understandably limited definitions of addiction have narrowed our understanding of what we are addressing. So, when I look back on my earlier (younger adult era) addressing of the matter of (what was being called) gestalt therapy being applied to (what was being understood as) addiction, I realize I see far more now and must share this.

OTHER GREATER MATTERS

There is a larger picture to call out and put on the hot seat. The client/patient and the treatment professional are reflecting each other in conceptual mirrors, present there as one in the same: we both share the human species' brain. What brand of (genetic and thus brain) programming we carry, our species carries, is not entirely clear. Who wrote this script, this design, that so adeptly weaves in our species' vulnerability to problem addiction? Did evolution itself program into us this glitch, this fatal flaw?

We can say, no, no, no, this is not an invading program, not an invasive intelligence, not a problem pattern drafting us to serve it. We want to say of course no one wrote this script, no one designed us this way. We want to say, of course this vulnerability to problem addiction programming is a random evolutionary or environmental accident.

I would like to say this, I would. However, I cannot say I am entirely certain this problem addiction patterning our species is experiencing is an accident of nature or evolution. However, if this problem programming is not an accident, what might it be? I return to this question in other books.[47]

If we allow ourselves, we feel, we sense, and "see" this problem addiction programming's ubiquitous presence. Hence, on some level, we must now be whispering, asking, or maybe even demanding, that the problem addiction program that is inhabiting us reveal itself, show its face: *unmask its disguise as us, as who we are, so we can see that this problem pattern inhabiting us is not us.* In so doing, we see the whole or at least the more whole picture. In this sense, what I am talking about in this book, *GESTALTING ADDICTION*, is not at all gestalt therapy, it is indeed:

THE
GESTALT.

---

[47] Refer to *UNVEILING THE HIDDEN INSTINCT* and *OVERRIDING THE EXTINCTION SCENARIO* listed in recommended reading at the end of this present book, *GESTALTING ADDICTION*.

CLOSING THE CIRCLE:
COMPLETING THE PICTURE

As a picture can at times be worth at least a thousand words, I am drawn back to the simple circle example that one of my earliest mentors, Gregory Bateson, had long ago explained to me. I still remember Bateson drawing this on the chalk board one day after the class he taught based on his book, *Steps to An Ecology of Mind*. Ever since that day in my young adulthood, much of my ongoing questioning of givens and of how these givens have been constructed (and or construed) stems from the realizations this one diagram generated and continues to generate in my mind. Those realizations are always affecting my thinking about what I am being told, and about what others tell me is "information," the "whole picture," and even "truth"....

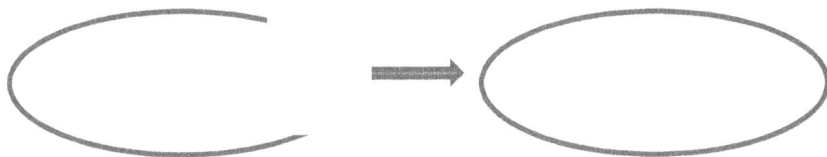

LAW OF CLOSURE:
THE FORM COMPLETION GESTALT

Basically, I look more to the underpinnings (dating at least as far back as those proposed by scientists in the late 1800s and early 1900s) of the notion of gestalt, than to the more modern therapies calling themselves gestalt and gestalt therapy. The underpinnings set forth by gestalt theorists attempted (and still attempt) to understand human perception and related thoughts and actions in terms of underlying processes, specifically underlying brain/perceptual processes, gestalts.

PERCEPTUAL ORGANIZATION
EXTENDED

These underpinnings consist of basic gestalt principles that involve perception itself and "laws of perceptual organization." The scientific origins of these underpinnings focused (and still do focus) primarily on ways the human eye sees visual elements. Central here is the basic notion that **the eye** (let me note here that this is of course more like the brain operating the eye than simply the eye)...

> ...completes the picture to depict
> the (or a) supposedly *whole* picture
> when all we ever can see is fragments of the whole.

I extend form completion beyond just visual elements here:

> This supposedly whole "complete" picture
> may be of surrounding physical reality,
> or can be a picture of ourselves,
> what is happening to or within us
> cognitively and emotionally and physically
> (such as cravings or other responses to
> triggers for falling back into and or
> remaining stuck in the trap, the double bind of
> the problem addiction pattern/cycle).

Given that we rarely if ever – in truth never – can see or perceive everything about anything -- about any object, event, interaction, emotion, etc. – then...

> ...our brains are constantly at work
> completing a picture of our reality for us,
> even a supposed picture of ourselves for us,
> even a picture of our patterns of addiction
> and their triggers, cues, elements, characteristics.

I therefore, in this book, *GESTALTING ADDICTION*, extend the basic gestalt principles of perception to a general approach to human experience (even the experience of being engaged in an addiction cycle/pattern) including perception, cognition, emotion, behavior, and yes, even addiction related sensations and behaviors.[48] My view is that we (our brains) are frequently if not always completing the picture so to speak, telling ourselves we see more of the whole picture (or situation or experience) than we do.

As nothing we see we see in its entirety, I suggest we, our brains, are always completing, or at least filling in, the picture of our experience of living and being. Somehow we find our way across town and through life, perceiving only parts of any pictures, places, things, events, experiences, emotions, etc.

We believe we are seeing a whole picture
when we are rarely if ever doing so.

Therefore we are likely
believing we are seeing
more than we are actually seeing.

---

[48] Of course, as I have explained, much of Human experience is based on genetic and then brain programming to respond to environmental cues and triggers, whether to implement healthy or to implement unhealthy patterns of behavior such as problem addiction behavior. And much of Human experience, including perception itself, is dictated by the patterns we are programmed to live within, and programmed to be addicted to. Therefore, when our brains are doing their ongoing form completion, reality estimation, we are being dictated to by this model of perception that tells us what our reality is whether or not this is our reality. Where problem addiction programming has invaded, then perception itself, even the form completion function, is affected, even controlled by the invading problem addiction programming.

WHEN
WHAT WE THINK IS THE WHOLE
IS GREATER THAN THE SUM OF
<u>WHAT WE THINK</u>
ARE ITS PARTS

Building on the notion that we are likely believing we are seeing more than we are actually seeing, we can say we are likely ...

> **believing that what we see**
> **is what we actually see,**
> **although it is not**.

Now, let's extend this idea to what we believe we know and feel:

> **We are likely believing we are knowing**
> **more than we actually know,**
> **and therefore behaving based on**
> **what we believe is happening,**
> **what we believe we are doing, feeling, sensing, craving,**
> **when this is not based on the whole picture and is**
> **only based on the brain's**
> **form completion and reality estimation functions.**

Thus, when we "know" (*believe we know*) what we perceive as being the whole, or the whole reality, or the whole experience, or the whole interaction, or the whole emotion, or the whole addiction pattern for that matter, we may or may not know the accuracy of what we know or feel is our reality. We may or may not even know the accuracy of what we know or feel is what is going on when we are being pulled back into repeating problem addiction cycles/patterns. The picture of our reality is being completed by our brain the way the brain form completes or closes this circle pictured again here….

A   **B**

perceived incoming data
represents part of the picture
or situation

the brain processes this data,
performs gestalt processes on this
incomplete perception
to "complete" this picture
or situation

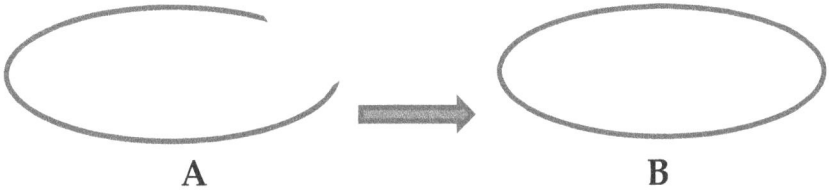

A   B

Now, think of broken Circle **A** above as an emotional or physical sensation/experience, or perhaps a craving cycle within an addiction pattern. What our brain's programming does with us as we experience/perceive this sensation and or craving is complete the picture above for us, as in Circle **B** above, and even…

CONFINE US TO THIS PICTURE:
SPILL US BACK INTO THE CYCLE WE ARE CAUGHT IN:

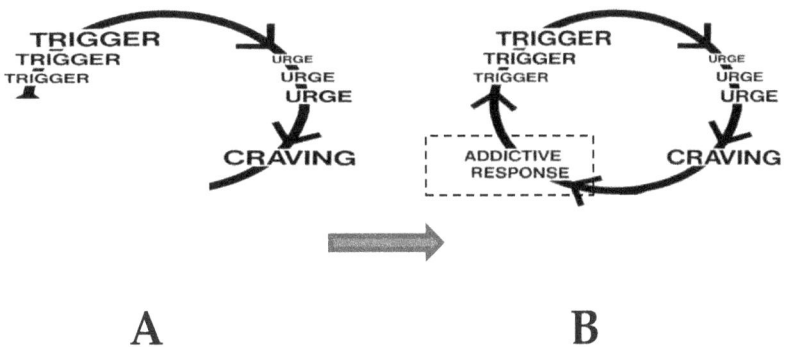

A   B

trigger to craving picture (A)
is completed by addictive response (B)
THIS (B) IS AN INFECTED GESTALT

The "whole" reality pattern/cycle we believe we feel or know or act out (Circle **B** above) is greater (but not necessarily more accurate or more healthy or more safe) than the whole reality we can construct (Circle **A** above) with the inherently incomplete information (data) we have with which to construct this "whole" picture of reality.

THE WHOLE IS NOT JUST THE SUM OF ITS PARTS
AND THE WHOLE KNOWS THIS

Take crowd mentality for example. One thousand people gather for a rock concert. Yes, each of them is an individual, so there are 1,000 individuals there, 1,000 incompletely perceived circles (Circle **A** on the previous page). Yet, there is also a crowd there (Circle **B**), a crowd with an energy and behavior of its own, more than simply that of 1,000 individuals (**A**'s). What we believe we see of our reality (**B**) is similar to this crowd. (See the Circle **B**'s pictured throughout this book.)

Consider a field. When we see this field of wildflowers, grasses, and shrubs, we may simply see the whole image rather than the individual plants within it. In fact, together these plants in that field form a mini-ecosystem that is far more complex than simply the addition of each plant (plant 1 plus plant 2 and so on) together. The whole is greater than the sum of its parts and indeed functions, survives, by being the whole greater than the sum of its parts.

We are however, left with both this truth, that the whole (B) is greater than the sum of its parts (A's), and this truth, which is that no whole (B) we perceive is the whole picture. This means that any form completion or reality estimation we have is still an incomplete (even inauthentic) picture and therefore not an authentic B. No matter what we think we perceive, see, feel, know, we are experiencing, we are still in the A category.

This is even the case when experiencing the problem addiction pattern cycle. No wonder we so readily miss the presence of the invasive problem addiction program. We are programmed to not see the tendrils of this presence working their way through us. (We never see the whole picture, never see an authentic whole Circle B.)

THE WHOLE IS
NOT JUST THE PARTS

As noted earlier, when the brain processes what the eye sees, it must, frequently even for survival purposes, rapidly see as much of the whole picture as it can. The brain must, far more rapidly than we can consciously manage to do (at this time in our brain's development or evolution) acquire, process, perform, a *gestalt* of the visual field.

Much of what our minds do with sensory and even other input is related, even parallel, to these basic visual (form completion) processes, which we can call **gestalts**. I list a few of these basic gestalt processes (or principles) below, following each with a "however" note suggesting that in these gestalts, *the brain can also misperceive or inaccurately conclude a perception into (perceived) existence*.

These "however" notes are not to question the value, even survival value, of the brain's perceptual gestalt processes. Rather, these notes are to also bring into focus the role of the gestalt processes in "controlling" perceptions (also in controlling sensations, emotions, and impulses regarding perceptions and thus responses to perceptions such as cravings), perhaps even leaving out or blocking or "denying" relevant information or alternative perceptions and options.

131

PATTERN PERCEPTION LAWS

These gestalt perception processes are pattern perception laws of gestalt psychology. And these are very important laws. However, we must know where these laws may break themselves. We may perceive/detect actual patterns. Or we may impose patterns where there are none, or complete patterns where we never see all there is to see. And we then proceed based on these estimated, incomplete, or even flawed perceptions of patterns....

Closure (Form Completion):
This is the process depicted by the circle closure **A→B** diagram appearing several times in this book. In this particular gestalt process, the human eye (and the brain operating it) "see" pictures missing details, then the brain provides or estimates the seemingly missing details to "complete" the picture or pattern. We tend to "see" things as whole even when they are not being perceived in their entirety. I note that, in generating this (apparent) closure, form completion (reality), this "completed" picture or pattern, the brain also selectively eliminates, and or selects to use or create details (such as missing or incorrect data) not legitimately contributing to forming an accurate completion.

> *However*, the elimination of details that do not fit the completion or closure the brain is generating may eliminate information needed for other and or more accurate, (and perhaps more healthy, more safe) conclusions, completions, gestalts.

Similarity:
The human eye (and of course the brain operating the human eye) "see" something, an object or image, and process what is seen by building a relationship to other elements within that visual field (such as in a view of a meadow), or within that design (such as in a view of a piece of art). Our brains process according to similarity,

telling us that things in the "field" that appear similar "go together."

> *However*, whether these "things" actually belong to some group or set, or "field," whether these "things" are actually similar in any way, is the question we want to ask. Do our brains impose on us a definition of our reality that is not actually our reality?

Continuation (Continuity):

The human eye (and the brain operating that human eye) "see" parts of a composition or a reality. From these parts, the brain creates a fluid connection between these parts, processing what is seen to "see" a continuous pattern or flow. We are thus more likely to perceive smooth flowing lines or forms rather than broken ones.

> *However*, the brain does this whether or not this continuous flow, this connection between these parts, this closure of broken lines/forms, actually depicts reality. Is this simply part of completing the broken circle, forming it into a full circle? What if the full circle is in actuality a broken circle while the brain gestalts it, closes it, to avoid the appearance of broken lines, incomplete forms, partial pictures?

Proximity:

The human eye and the brain operating it can "see" things, objects, shapes, that are near each other as belonging to the same group of things, objects, or shapes—even when these objects or shapes are distinctly different. Things that appear to belong together based on some variable are then perceived as belonging to the same group. For example, letters appearing on this page without spaces between them are likely separate words. Their proximity allows us to read the words on this page.

However, we must ask: how frequently is the grouping based on this proximity erroneous, or at least a vast over generalization, losing information during this generalizing?

Figure/Ground:

The human eye and the brain operating the human eye "separate" figures from their background, and in processing what is "seen," the eye/brain isolates objects or patterns from the data around them or in their background. How we interpret sensory information is largely dependent on how we distinguish between figure and (back)ground.

> *However*, when an item is identified as something to be distinguished from a background that is identified, are we to accept that this object and this background are the actual object and actual background? How much information may be lost in the process? What other perspective might also be relevant?

Symmetry (Order):

The human eye and the brain operating that human eye, upon "seeing" something that may not be symmetrical or may not be easy to comprehend (due to its newness or its disorganization or its complexity), imposes an order, a symmetry, a logic upon/into the perception. The brain allows us to take in information that may be too complex to understand, by organizing, perhaps even (over?) simplifying this information.

> *However*, the gestalt process of imposing an "order" on information coming in allows the brain's control function to recategorize, even override, even exclude what may be useful data (or useful data priority). Where does the raw data go? Do we have a way to see what our brain has processed (and processed out) for us? How do we know what our brain has excluded?

GESTALT
PSYCHOLOGY AND THEORY

Gestalt psychology formed itself around early theories of visual perception that emerged in the early 20th century, providing the foundation for the modern study of perception. These theories regarding visual perception explained that *the mind/brain fills in what is missing in what it sees*.

For example, we see a moving object, or a movie, as flowing rather than a series of separate movements or screens. This *Phi Phenomenon* explains the *illusion of movement* when what is seen is a series of still pictures in quick succession. We perceive objects within larger wholes. The mind forms a global perception, a "global whole." And this whole is more than only the sum of its parts. Yet, who monitors this form or whole completion for accuracy and veracity?

ANSWER TO
CHAOS?

Gestalt psychology is understood and applied differently in different settings and fields, and by different professionals. However, there is an overarching sense that gestalt psychology seeks to develop "meaningful" understandings, or at least "meaningful perceptions" in what may appear to be chaotic situations.

That gestalt actually succeeds in serving as an antidote, or perhaps an answer to the sense of chaos, is subject to various views. No definite conclusion has been arrived at, as there is no consensus regarding chaos, its nature, its existence, its dangers or discomforts, and its solutions if any are required.

OLD SCHOOL GESTALT
BEING OVERRIDDEN

For decades, likely even more than a century, a central position at play in gestalt psychology, or at least in its underlying theory of perception, was that all the basic principles of gestalt (as noted earlier: Closure, Similarity, Continuity, Proximity, Figure/Ground, Symmetry, even the Phi Phenomenon) are **innate** in that the human mind/brain has an *"innate* disposition to perceive patterns" in particular ways.

Old school gestalt psychology maintained the notion that the basic gestalt laws are innate and not experience-derived. However, more recent research has established what some describe as the opposite finding:

**experience most definitely
influences perception.**

Today this sounds quite obvious to many of us who have grown up personally and professionally in an entirely different era (far past the time of the 19th and early to mid 20th century, for example). Of course experience influences how we "see" things, how we feel about what we "see," and how we respond to what we "see."

PRE-ATTENTIVE PROCESSING
VS. ATTENTIVE PROCESSING

Although that original innate basis stance caused gestalt theory to be misunderstood, even criticized, for quite some time, new understandings of the notion that the whole is more than the sum of its parts, and that yes, experience is a key element in perception, have taken center stage. Moreover, this shift in thinking is ever more supported by ever further emerging addiction related research in areas such as *attention* and *attentional bias*.[49]

Of note here are even basic attention functions. For example, "pre-attentive" visual processing occurs in visual (sensory) memory without our conscious involvement in this process. This pre-attentive processing takes some 500 milliseconds. However, at least conceptually, this *leaves the other end of the spectrum open to us*, to our consciously sorting and/or differentiating data to both classify these data and then to respond to these. Of course, this involves our being conscious of what we are processing, or at least our consciously processing some of what we process. What actually takes places is largely below our ***conscious awareness***,[50] as I like to call it. I add the term, *aware* to *conscious*, so as to differentiate between various levels of consciousness, few of which we are consciously engaged in.

Pre-Attentive Processing →→→
Attentive Processing →→→
Aware ***Attentive* Processing***

Of course, the scientific term, "attentive processing," does not refer specifically to the ***aware*** attentive processing and thus its ***aware conscious*** processing I have suggested* in the spectrum above and elsewhere further set forth and defined.[51]

Of note is the discussion regarding *attention and consciousness*, even the tension between attention and consciousness, in several fields,

---

[49] See for example the volume on *Psychobiological Profiles* in the *INTERNATIONAL COLLECTION ON ADDICTIONS,* noted on reading list at the end of this book.
[50] I further define and discuss ***aware consciousness*** in *UNVEILING THE HIDDEN INSTINCT.*
[51] See reading list at the end of this book.

some of which note that, "...not all forms of attention produce the same kind of consciousness; not all forms of consciousness are produced by the same kind of attention; ... top down attention and consciousness are distinct phenomena that need not occur together."[52]

As we are constantly dealing with data coming at and into us, our brain addresses much of this far more rapidly and efficiently than we consciously can. At the other end of the spectrum is "attentive" processing, in this case attentive visual processing, which involves searching through the data, or at least searching through objects or items in a set or series.

STILL AND RACING WATERS
RUN DEEP

We know our addiction programming runs deep. Much of this programming operates out of our awareness. What we do consciously experience of this programming to be addicted is just the tip of the iceberg — and just an incomplete picture of even that tip of the iceberg.

So much complex processing, complex work relating to how we operate, function, feel, and think, takes place on the unconscious level, where our aware consciousness, our aware attentive consciousness, does not go. There, where our aware consciousness does not go, a vast array of neural mechanisms are operating at all times, or poised to operate at all times. Some of what is generated or initiated there, deep inside our mind/brain — perceptions and

---

[52] See discussion of this and related matters in Giorgio Marchetti, *Against the view that consciousness and attention are fully dissociable*. Frontiers in Psychology. 2012, 3:36.

resulting impulses, thoughts, wants, needs, for example--surface in our aware consciousness.

And the reverse direction is also the case. What appears to take place in the realm of our aware consciousness makes its way into the sub- and un- conscious. Indeed, data/information about the experience that is experienced by the aware consciousness makes its way deeper in, to the sub- and un- conscious levels. Experience thus affects what takes place deep down in the sub- and un-conscious recesses of our minds/brains. Therefore, even there, in these recesses of our minds/brains so far from our conscious awareness, environment affects the processing of information and perception.

Environment is also at work on other mental functions and processes, such as, what is commonly referred to in the addiction field as *denial*. Denial offers a powerful example of the interaction between biology and environment, an interaction we are frequently not aware is taking place. (See an antidote to what some call denial in parts of the **Going Conscious Process** I talk about in the chapters of *Part Six*.)

Clearly, denial involves not paying attention, or trying not to pay attention, to important information. So, let's examine denial (in the next chapter, *Chapter 9*), see what is taking place when we are (told we are) "in denial"....

Part Four:

Looking
Beyond Known Addiction
For the Actual Addiction

Dr. Angela®

"I'm looking for the *Light*."

9
Denial and Confrontation: Recipe for What?

Denial is not just a river in Egypt, as the popular adage suggests. Dictionaries tell us that *denial* is: the act of declaring something untrue; refusal to admit the truth; also, the *denial* of rights or privileges or some other status. Synonyms for *denial* include disavowal, dismissal, refusal to acknowledge, disbelief. Psychology tells us that *denial* is a defense mechanism, that *denial* avoids addressing or confronting a personal matter or problem by denying its reality, denying its existence. Some will say that *denial* is lying. Others include forms of avoidance, non-compliance, and resistance under the umbrella of denial.

Denial has become such a go-to description of so many complex attitudes and behaviors that what *denial* actually is has been obscured. We can see this in some areas of addiction treatment and addiction therapy. In fact, some treatment professionals shortchange both themselves and their work with persons who are addicted when they jump almost automatically to *denial* as a catch all for what is taking place in the mind/brain of the addicted person.

MANY FORMS OF DENIAL
MAY BE FORMS OF SOMETHING ELSE

The myriad *denial*s explicitly referred to, or implicitly implied, in treatment, therapy, peer group, and other addiction focused settings risk some degree of overgeneralization. And at times, the risk is profound enough that a miscasting of addiction and recovery processes can take place. Too often, *denial* is being stretched too far, at times being used as a convenience or shorthand or labeling habit, other times being used out of misunderstanding. Misuse of (the concept of) *denial* results in mis-addressing many details of addiction and its wide and varied range of emotions, attitudes, and behaviors.

What is so readily labelled as *denial* may be far more complex than this simple label can address, may have elements beyond *simply denying* such as:

- Forming attitude, opinion,
            without full information regarding what is true.
- Believing that what is not true is true, and what is true is not true.
- Avoiding the truth while knowing pieces of the truth.
- Avoiding the truth while knowing the "whole" truth.
- Claiming something other than the truth is true.
- Lying about what is true.

AND OR...
- Being *unable* to recognize the truth.
- Disconnecting or dissociating from the truth.
- Inability to process information and emotion that would allow
            knowing the truth.

In clinical settings, such as addiction treatment, or group therapy, or individual psychotherapy, what is being called (or treated as, whether or not precisely labeled as) *denial* appears rather frequently. Professionals and peers exhibit a range of responses to this *denial* and or **perceived** *denial*.

In addiction treatment environments, all too frequently accusations such as, "You're not telling the truth, that's your denial talking," are shouted or at least asserted in some confrontational way. This broad brush approach to this thing that gets called *denial* is not always correct or useful, and at times is far off base.

MISUSE OF CONFRONTATION

The *misuse of confrontation* can at times be quite damaging, as can accusation of denial when what is taking place may be far more complex than denial. For example, the lower part of the above list of some reasons for, or causes of, what is called denial includes these: being unable to recognize the truth; disconnecting or dissociating from the truth; inability to process information and emotion that would allow knowing the truth. These and other brain/mind conditions may or may not be present when an addicted person is not agreeing to or seeing the truth about her or his problem addiction. That individual may or may not be "in denial" per se. *As I have noted in earlier chapters, the problem addiction programming seeks to sustain itself and therefore may disguise its agenda behind what appears to be its host's — our — denial.*

What may appear to onlookers to be simple denial may have other dimensions. Confronting the client or patient with implied or outright accusation of denial may not address what is actually taking place, and may be counterproductive.

**We must keep in mind that
problem addiction is a chronic brain disease.
An element of this chronic brain disease is
what may appear to be denial.**

DENIAL AT WILL?

Is denial actually denial when it is not taking place at will? If the individual's brain simply does not, or even cannot, recognize or respond to information, does this mean the individual is denying this information? Does confronting that individual regarding his or her so called denial actually help? While the reply is yes in many instances, there is also a no, not at all times in everyone.

To hold everyone, including all patients and clients, "responsible" for their denial (if any) incorrectly assumes they are "in denial" about something, and that they are in *denial at will*.

Indeed, some in the field of addiction have been preoccupied with what is generally called "denial," which is described as the tendency to ignore, or *deny*, information. People who are addicted to drugs and alcohol (again, alcohol which itself is a drug), and or other non-drug behaviors such as gambling, frequently exhibit what *appears* to be the tendency to engage in some form of what may appear to onlookers to be *self deception*. This *self deception* is generally viewed as lying to oneself.

Describing (literally or just by subtle implication) what addicted persons engage in as a form of *self deception* is an over simplification, a subjective labeling of something far more complex than this. The term, *self deception*, suggests that there is a *will to deceive oneself*, a will to be in denial, a will to lie to others about addiction behaviors and addiction attitudes, perhaps even a will to be lying to oneself.

This is NOT to say self deception, even denial, are always incorrect descriptions. This IS to say that, when there is a problem addiction pattern, the brain and its functions may be affected or invaded, even subsumed, by the problem addiction programming. And, it is this programming that presents the *appearance of deception and denial in its host* to hide behind and to fortify itself. Remember,

WE ARE NOT
THE PROBLEM ADDICTION PROGRAMMING,
WE ARE THE HOST OF THIS PROGRAMMING.

This does not relieve us of the responsibility to do everything we can to address and turn back this invasive programming.

Self deception is frequently labeled as denial. Accusations of *willing* self deception are too frequently judgmental, accusatory, imparting some degree of moral judgement. I have seen so many people working in addiction treatment and therapy actively confront patients and clients, addicts, telling them they are lying to themselves and others, insisting that they are "in denial." No matter how this is played and replayed in our discussion of this confrontation, there is some form of judgment embedded in this accusation. Frequently, no matter how it is described, this is the moral judgment I refer to here.

Yet, *we must ask*: When is self deception unwilling or unintentional self deception? Could the invasive addiction pattern program be disguising itself via self deception? How would we know if anything we "know" about this is perhaps only self deception, or maybe the opposite of self deception? Simply put, the invasive programming seeks to obfuscate the truth, hiding the truth about what is really happening.

The invasive addiction pattern program is holding its hosts trapped in its addiction cycle patterns, so trapped that really seeing what is happening is very difficult to do from within the trap.

Those of us who work with those trapped in those addiction cycle patterns must try to see this, and also try to see how very pulled into these patterns we can also be, even when we are certain we are standing outside clients' addiction cycle patterns.

NO LONGER MORAL JUDGEMENT

Now, we tend to tell ourselves that "modern" views of addiction no longer carry the moral judgement so common in earlier attitudes toward addicted persons, for example, views that said addiction was a "moral failing." The "moral failing" view was that: (a) the addicted person had somehow deliberately chosen to use the drug or drink the alcohol (alcohol is a drug) again and again, despite the consequences; and (b) therefore this was engaging in this undesirable behavior *at will.*

IS THE DENIAL
SOMEHOW AT WILL,
A CHOICE THAT IS MADE
VOLUNTARILY?

We cannot dissect the brain molecule by molecule or even synapse by synapse to know precisely what is taking place when someone is (or is said to be) in denial, or doing any form of *lying* to him or herself, or to others. Yes, there are studies of the human brain showing that **brain changes take place when lies are told.** In fact, some research shows that (a) the brain (generally its amygdala) generates a negative feeling (such as shame or guilt) when the person is telling a lie; however, (b) ongoing lying, habitual or pathological lying, can desensitize the brain to (the "a" here) its original response to telling a lie; and in fact (c) this **desensitization to lying** can even lead to telling bigger and bigger lies.[53]

---

[53] Center for Ethical Leadership, *What Dishonesty Does to Your Brain.* University of Notre Dame, 2019.
<<https://ethicalleadership.nd.edu/news/what-dishonesty-does-to-your-brain-why-lying-becomes-easier-and-easier/>>
Neil Garret, et. al., *The brain adapts to dishonesty.* Nature Neuroscience, Volume 19. pp.1727-1732(2016).

Given that the brain can be desensitized to lying, let's ask this: Does an addicted person engaging in so called denial and or self deception grow less and less sensitive to his or her own denial and self deception? Is it possible that brain changes stop the self from stopping its own denial about its own addiction behaviors and addiction attitudes? *I say this is the problem addiction programming at work, protecting itself, with its host's — our — speaking for that programming by not knowing or telling the truth.*

If addiction itself changes the brain, and if addiction itself causes the addicted person to be so addicted to a drug that using that drug is desired over not using this drug, what other *desensitizations* are taking place in the addicted person's brain? I ask this because we must ask:

**At what point
does the addicted person
lose control over
his/her brain's response to
lying about (denying) his or her addiction?**

TRUTH OR DARE

Telling of the truth, the whole truth and nothing but the truth, to others can be challenging for some, especially in the face of a problem addiction. *Indeed, since we never see the whole picture for all that it truly is, since we never know everything, then any truth we may tell is an approximation.* And there are other complications. The other person being told the truth may not want to hear the truth, may not like the truth, may not believe what is being called the truth. Familial, social, even societal resistances to truth can make telling the truth a challenge. Now, combine these factors with the invasive problem addiction programming (see *Chapter 13*), and we see the addicted person almost lost in the shuffle.

In many cases, *the still greater challenge is to tell the truth to oneself.* Here is where the truth comes face to face with any internal and or external resistances to, or filters of, or infected gestalts distorting, this truth.

Telling the truth to oneself can present various challenges such as: (a) There may be learned resistances to the truth, some reflecting familial or social or societal factors as noted above, especially when these factors or influences have been internalized by the person telling the truth (in which case these resistances are no longer entirely external); or, (b) There may brain resistances to truth such as (*) the brain having been desensitized to lying, as described earlier in this chapter, or (**) the brain having a program, a neural and biochemical programming, to filter out some truths, some realizations that may be deemed by the brain to be too much for the person to consciously handle, to cope with, to live with.

Once we see how fragile the truth can be (that is if there is a truth to be told), how susceptible truth is to external and internal influences, even to perception itself,[54] truth becomes ever more fluid, ever more elusive, ever more vulnerable. (*Is a form completion a truth? Is any truth any more than the result of a form completion process?*)

---

[54] Brain functions and processes (such as **attentional bias**) can be profoundly affected by problem addictions. See chapters discussing this in *INTERNATIONAL COLLECTION ON ADDICTIONS*, as well as in *TRANSCENDING ADDICTION*. Refer to reading list at the end of this book.

And where there is a problem addiction affecting many cognitive and emotional, even perceptual, functions, the addicted individual is *not entirely free to exercise free will*, and not free to fully and clearly recognize the *difference between free will and controlled will* as a result of external and internal influences and factors, even addictions.

So here is my question: *When the brain of the addicted individual is virtually being controlled by the addiction, how much freedom to perceive the truth, and then to tell the truth, to even feel the value of the truth, does the addicted individual have?*

Telling the truth to oneself (and to others) is a big step in the face of the heavy control a problem addiction pattern program has over the mind. Yet, in the face of a heavy addiction, truth becomes elusive, surfacing and receding, forming and reforming, disguising itself as so many things, including as truth itself. Yet we, *the host of this programming not to know* what is true and what is not true, may be too far from knowing to discern effectively.

This leaves us having to ask (rather than decide this and judge the addicted person based on what we have been taught is going on in that person's mind): How much say does the addicted person have in terms of free will, in terms of truth telling, in terms of facing and fighting the addiction pattern program, in standing up to ...

the denial
the addiction itself
calls for,
even demands?

GESTALTING DENIAL

Given that we are all form completing, revealing, gestalting pieces of our realities to form whole pictures of our realities, or what appear to be whole pictures of our realities, we are all engaged in our brain's figure completion processes – figure completion, sequence of event completion, story completion, emotion completion, addiction cycle completion, etc. As I have noted earlier in this book and explained in depth in other books, our brains are telling us what we know, or at least telling us what we think or feel we know.

So our brains, under direction of the invasive problem addiction programming, are *orchestrating* any denial, resistance, even self deception, we express. How much control do we actually have over our brains? This remains the question.

10
Seeing Past Addiction
And
Addiction Treatment Paradigms

Addiction wears many faces, far more than we see, far more than we admit to, far more than we understand. Ultimately, the brain function to form patterns of behavior, many relatively automatic, is a natural and even useful function. Aren't we glad we form healthy habits such as automatically stopping at red traffic lights? What we do and know and learn utilizes the brain's programming to do so.

Where problem addictions emerge is where the brain function to program itself so effectively runs so far afield, so far out of line, and programs its host to repeat a problem behavior over and over even in the face of increasing harm to self or others. **The problem addiction pattern program is designed to confuse both the perception of and the response to positive and negative feedback and reinforcement**. The problem addiction program is designed to bundle these opposing reinforcements together, to blur and confuse them, to reprioritize and even alter awareness of self protection and self harm. **Now the brain's reward center rewards not only what is healthy and safe, but also what is harmful**, as the problem addiction pattern program has woven itself into the reward circuit, distorted the reward function for its own purposes.

> **Self protection is corrupted,**
> **and now used by the addiction program**
> **to protect itself and its own agenda,**
> **not protect its host — not protect us.**

Yet, this running awry leading us to program in, and stay trapped within, problem addiction patterns is not a sign of a person being morally unfit or "bad" (as earlier views of addicted persons all too frequently held). Nor is this a sign that a person is in so called denial. So much more is taking place.

Fortunately, the old moral judgement view of the addict as someone morally compromised has retreated, at least overtly. As I explain in the previous chapter, there do remain elements of moral judgement present in the *implicit accusation and judgement subtext* at times present in the confrontation of what is said to be the addicted person's denial. (When I say this, I am not seeking to eliminate all direct addressing of denial in working with addicted persons, not at all. What I am saying, as explained in the previous chapter, is that denial is complex, and has biological underpinnings far deeper than simply the expression of denial.)

EVEN QUESTIONING THE BRAIN DISEASE MODEL AS BEING THE WHOLE STORY

The chronic brain disease model has largely shifted the addiction treatment field away from the old view of the "addict" as being one who is morally compromised. The brain disease model of problem addiction has arisen with the growth of biomedical research technologies such as gene sequencing and magnetic resonance imaging (MRI). While technologies allowing us to understand ever more about the mechanisms and nature of addiction are valuable, these in themselves do not give us the whole picture.

> **Anything we say about addiction is simply a still shot of a moving picture. Even the "more modern" brain disease model is not giving us the whole picture.**

BUT WHO
IS THE ADDICT?

In our times, so many have their answers to and treatments for what they call "addiction" and for whom they call the "addict." It seems that almost every field has had something to say about this condition so commonly called "addiction." And no matter how many forms of addiction treatment and addiction focused therapy/psychotherapy rise to the occasion, no matter how many millions of persons are treated for addiction, co-addiction, and related behaviors, this thing we call addiction is still with us, even taking on new forms and faces each passing day.

NOT FULLY UNDERSTANDING ADDICTION
WHILE TREATING IT

Also in our times, and unfortunately so, there are those who do not fully understand what addiction is (including but not limited to the dimensions of addiction I address in this book) who nevertheless treat (or otherwise address if they are not professionally licensed to treat) addiction. Whether it be well meaning licensed professionals or well meaning certified counselors, or well meaning peer group members and sponsors, or others, the general naivete regarding what I call addiction programming of the human brain can result in mistaken, confusing, and sometimes harmful approaches and guidance. All too often, when an addicted individual relapses, this individual is told (often rather harshly) that the relapse occurred as a result of his or her denial or at least non-compliance with recovery programming. Denial as well as non-compliance are the catch all concepts for so much not understood regarding addiction (as noted in the previous chapter).

There are also those professionals who are telling themselves (and others) that they have *the* answers to addiction. And again, all too frequently, these professionals are telling clients and patients that if they relapse or "use again," if they do not stop their "addictive behavior," this is the result of their denial or their lack of adherence to the prescribed program (as a result of their denial or laziness or noncompliance of some sort—all hinging in some way on their denial).

The addicted individual's "willing" non-compliance with doctor's or program's orders or directives is "blamed" or held responsible for his or her not succeeding in staying out of her or his problem addiction pattern. How convenient it is to blame the victim, the person who is the victim of our brain's inherent programming to become addicted to healthy and unhealthy behavioral patterns.[55] (In addiction treatment, it appears too frequently, this all too ready approach: blame the victim for the disease affecting the victim.)

Let me therefore offer a word to Readers here, which is simply that any one source of treatment claiming to have all the answers and solutions is likely not offering fully effective or even fully honest treatment. As I prefer to refrain from describing so many esteemed colleagues as professionally or even intellectually uninformed or even dishonest, I will instead simply say that there appears to be the presence of some degree of (perhaps understandable) short sightedness in these fields and among some professionals claiming absolute expertise in these fields.

---

[55] See recommended reading at the end of this book listing publications such as *UNVEILING THE HIDDEN INSTINCT* and *OVERRIDING THE EXTINCTION SCENARIO*, where I discuss in greater depth how the matter of the brain taking on habits, even addictions, is natural and likely was evolved for survival purposes, and that with problem addictions, the brain's pattern building functions are running awry.

11
Cautionary Notes on
Medically Assisted Treatment (MAT)
and
Psychedelically Assisted Treatment (PAT)

Everything that can be done to assist persons afflicted with problem addiction patterning must be done. Yes? Of course, at least two factors affect this *everything that can be done must be done* view: (a) not knowing what is *absolutely guaranteed* to work, and work without adding harm; and, (b) not finding a way to address the societal bars on various treatments that can or do work.

MAT
CAN BE LIFE SAVING

As noted by Kim Borwick, DrugRehab.com Editor, "For more than five decades, research has confirmed the benefits of medication-assisted treatment for people recovering from addiction. But lack of education, antiquated beliefs that abstinence is the only true recovery, and the precarious balance of power between clinicians, researchers, politicians, and people on the front lines of addiction have caused millions of Americans to be denied access to life-saving treatment."[56]

---

[56] Kim Borwick, *Myths fueling the stigma of medication-assisted treatment.* <https://www.drugrehab.com/featured/the-myths-and-misconceptions-of-medication-assisted-treatment/>

Certainly advances in the treatment of addiction, including state of the art MAT, should be available to all suffering problem addictions. Unfortunately, too many do not have the resources or opportunities to utilize these treatments. We are seeing the consequences of this limited access on both personal and societal levels.

MAT
CAN ALSO BE MIS-ADMINISTERED

It is essential those prescribing MATs are highly trained MAT specialists, and are always on alert for the effects of their MATs. Medically assisted treatment (MAT) is indeed proving valuable, even life saving in so many cases, however not in all cases. There are too many instances where MAT is being self administered, and or professionally administered (wrongly, or over administered) with other than positive effects. (There are even suggested self administer MATs available globally, online, by mail order.)

I advocate for great and highly informed care in administering both psychopharmacological (medically assisted treatment of addiction or MAT) and psychedelic approaches (the use of hallucinogens, etc. in treatments of addiction and of other conditions, what I describe as PAT). I also strongly differentiate between MAT (medically assisted treatments) and PAT (psychedelic assisted treatments).

There is still a great need for far more research on not only short term effects but also on **long term effects (the lasting brain and life changing effects)** of such MAT and also PAT treatments. We are talking about brain changes here, externally induced (via medications and or psychedelics) changes in the brain, changes that are generally irreversible and may have long term unforeseen effects. As these are treatments being administered to "treat" addiction which itself can cause irreversible brain changes, those administering MATs and PATs must proceed with great care. I am already seeing, now for several years, clients coming to me to get help with the effects of MATs and PATs they have been or are in the process of being prescribed and administered by both licensed and unlicensed professionals and others.

DEVELOPMENTS
IN THE ADDICTION FIELD:
BETTER LIVING
THROUGH PAT CHEMISTRY?

Before I continue this discussion, let me distinguish between MAT and PAT approaches. While both approaches are utilizing "drugs" to affect the minds of persons experiencing addiction conditions, MATs are generally prescriptions of government approved and scheduled medicines. PATs are less regulated, or are indeed regulated however being used in and outside of regulatory and even professional supervision. Additionally, the impact on the mind of psychedelic compounds is even less measured for *long term effects* than are MATs.

Some developments in the addiction treatment field must be watched closely for the tendency to sing praises of particular approaches when they do not address the full range of realities addicted people face. For example, the psychedelic treatments for addiction that have emerged (or re-emerged) must be closely watched for potential misuses of these at times themselves addictive treatments.

While this is not a review of the pros and cons of such "treatment" for addiction, of note here is that there are indeed both pros and cons to the psychedelic treatments and psychedelic psychotherapies. Those administering such treatments and therapies must advise clients and patients before beginning and at all points along the way, of the pros and cons of and the unknowns in this work.

The use of psychedelic drugs in treating psychiatric/psychological matters/problems such as depression, anxiety, and addiction has been found in some research to be "effective" in some cases.[57] Of course, the way "effective" is defined and how long this "effectiveness" is measured remains largely subjective, as are most definitions.

Those questioning or even warning about this psychedelic "medicine" note the almost hypervigilance of many of the advocates of psychedelic medicine, the at times intensely optimistic views of its value, even in many instances views a little too euphoric[58] to appear entirely professionally motivated, views sometimes even saying that psychedelic "medicine" is a good response to "almost every malady."

Those who are speaking out with warnings regarding the use of psychedelics to treat addiction and other psychological/psychiatric conditions are noting that these drugs actually do induce brain

---

[57] These drugs include but are not limited to MDMA, LSD, psilocybin, ayahuasca, etc., and ever new and emerging "designer" drugs.

[58] This being described as: "a euphoria similar to the enchantment found among persons using or even addicted to various 'addictive' drugs, and even drugs not viewed as addictive, for example MDMA (3,4 methylene-dioxymethamphetamine or methylenedioxy-methylamfetamine)." Note that the US National Institute on Drug Abuse (NIDA) states that "regular MDMA use produces adaptations in the serotonin and dopamine systems that are associated with substance use disorder and related behaviors, such as increased impulsivity." [*Advancing Addiction Science, Is MDMA Addictive?* NIDA 9/2017:1.p.1]
<https://www.drugabuse.gov/publications/research-reports/mdma-ecstasy-abuse/mdma-addictive>

changes such as stimulating neuron cell growth and increasing neuronal connections (an argument proponents of psychedelic medicine also use). The matter of inducing brain changes in clients and patients, and doing so under these circumstances, may for some experts, call into question the approaches of at least some of the proponents of this use of psychedelics.

IATROGENIC OR
TRULY BETTER LIVING
THROUGH CHEMISTRY?

Relapse reduction has been the banner and the evidence based claim of medically assisted treatment of addiction (MAT). Effective MAT has evolved over the decades. From the first methadone programs of the early 1970s, and then on to the methadone maintenance programs successfully addressing a significant percent of heroin addiction, to OUD (opioid use disorder) treatments with their documented results, to the MAT of other substance use disorders (SUDs), there is good reason to make MAT widely available. Of course, again we want to proceed with care, and with due diligence.

How can anyone really claim to know precisely what are the full and precise short and long term effects of induced brain changes at the cellular, as well as psychological, social, life path, and other levels? Who can and should be responsible for applying psychoactives to induce brain and personality changes in other persons simply because that person has trusted the health or mental health care provider (or some other figure such as the shaman or drug dealer) to induce these changes? We can and must set high standards for training and certifying persons conducting both MAT and PAT (including PAT's psychedelically assisted therapy, treatment, guiding, and or other work).

12
Confronting Addiction:
Addiction, Reveal Yourself

We humans continue to struggle with the basic nature of our brains. What parts of our less than healthy behaviors can be changed, improved, helped in some way? What level of "help," assistance, treatment, intervention, etc., actually helps? We do best to continually measure effects and outcomes (both short and long term outcomes), as well as to continually revise and improve the outcome measures we do use.

We as a society, even as a species, continue to struggle with the matter of "addiction" to something, to drugs, substances, or even to more general areas such as behaviors and emotions. Fortunately, we are working with an ever increasing amount of research and experience in the health and mental health care, and addiction treatment, fields. Science, medicine, and health/mental health care is ever more aware of the nature of compulsive, habitual, and addiction behaviors.

Yes, these days we do know more. And we think we do know more. But more about what? I have to ask this question again and again. As I continue to say here in *GESTALTING ADDICTION* and in other of my books, ***the human brain appears to have an agenda of its own. DO WE UNDERSTAND WHAT THIS MEANS?***

TIP OF THE ADDICTION ICEBERG

Reader, after so many years, decades, of looking at, working with, treating, studying, analyzing, drug/alcohol as well as various nondrug/behavioral addictions and their many faces, I have come to the conclusion that: what we believe we now know about this thing we call *addiction* is more than ever merely the tip of the iceberg. In essence, the more we know, the more we know we still do not know. This is because the human brain is so complex, practically an infinite universe of electrical, neural, and biochemical (among other – many I say are still not yet defined) events and functions.

My experience is that we are still on the frontier of addiction and its treatment. To say we have arrived is to deny the reality that we are still just beginning. New and even as yet unforeseen addictions, new aspects of brain functions (and their programmings) driving addictions, new treatments and therapies, will continue to emerge. Get ready. Our addict-ability will remain with us, within our programming, and must be ever monitored.

I have found problem addiction to take on its own persona, either in the eye of the beholder or in its own eye. Addiction develops, grows, structures, feeds, fuels, rationalizes, itself within the social, cultural, community, family, psychological, spiritual, biological, neurological, genetic, political, and other environments we provide it (or it provides us).

**To confront addiction,
we must call it out from within
the recesses of our lives, our worlds, ourselves.**

ADDICTION,
REVEAL YOURSELF

OK, addiction, reveal yourself for who and what you are in all your complexity, in all your disguises. Complete the picture, reveal your true and whole nature, and your actual agenda:

GESTALT YOURSELF,
ADDICTION.

And addiction, where you still withhold so many of your truths, I call you to come forward to further reveal yourself as what/who you truly are. Reveal the whole picture of yourself.

And addiction, in truth you do remain cryptic, even incomplete, in the picture of yourself you present. I call upon you to complete the picture, to connect the dots for us, to *gestalt yourself.*

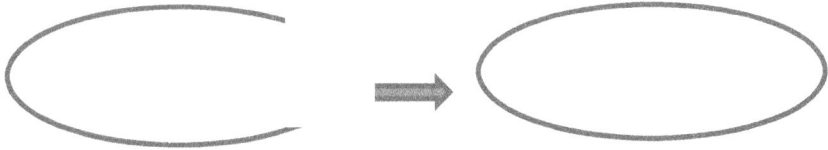

what addiction appears to be → **what addiction actually is**

Our brains are programmed to have us (or have our brain programming itself) grow addicted to convenient, safe, even survival related behaviors. We of course have deeply ingrained impulse driven instincts that protect us such as the fight, flight, and freeze reflexes. We also have the ability to form (acquire) healthy new habits while living such as stopping at red lights.

However, and I will say this again here, our brain's programmable nature is running far awry. *(And I will ask again: or is it? Could it be that our programming is right on track, with its goal of holding us bound to being highly addict-able life forms?*[59]*)* Our brain programming is far

---

[59] Again see, *UNVEILING THIS HIDDEN INSTINCT* and *OVERRIDING THE EXTINCTION SCENARIO,* as listed in recommended reading at the end of this present book, *GESTALTING ADDICTION.*

too frequently forming problem, even dangerous, patterns of addiction, threatening lives, even killing too many afflicted persons.

GESTALTING ADDICTION

I am offering this book, GESTALTING ADDICTION, to start the process of **gestalting addiction** itself, to reveal addiction in its actual context(s), to call addiction out of hiding, out from behind its masks to show us who it truly is.

WHAT GESTALT <u>IS</u>

Although in this book I do develop concepts that are relevant in gestalt therapy as well as in other therapy, this book is not so much about what some professionals may know as "gestalt therapy." Rather, this book is more about what gestalt *is*, or can be, (and with this, what addiction is, or can be understood to be).

Yes, I have spent many hours in rooms conducting individual and group therapy, gestalt and other forms of therapy, with persons seeking to find more out about themselves and their feelings, and/or their behaviors, including their problem addictions. It has become clear to me that conducting any particular form of therapy "on" or "with" clients is not always the appropriate approach, especially when we are talking about habitual and addicted conditions and behaviors. Yes, I can hear some of my colleagues stopping me here, telling me I must not decry therapy itself as it has, they say, "helped so many people." Of course, I do agree, yet I want to add a few notes here....

First, I want to note that if therapy has helped, it has helped people *help themselves*. Whether it be the therapy or the psychotherapist, what of the client's own change may be taking place is within the client, not outside the client, not within the therapy or the psychotherapist, as these are not within the client. (Sure, the therapist may also change in doing this work, yet this is not the client's change, it is the therapist's change.) All too frequently, the therapist takes credit for the work the client does (often while the client, when not doing well, is blamed by that same therapist for not following recovery directives).

Second, and most important to me as I share in this book, is the understanding that when we work with a single or a room full of what some will call "addict/s" and who I prefer to call "person/s experiencing addiction, which is all of us," we are not working with people who have problems per se. We are doing something else, if we are doing something effective, if we are doing something that is *for our clients*:

We are working with our clients (who are experiencing problem addictions) as they work with themSELVES, with their own brains/minds/bodies to identify, speak to, and break free of invasive problem addiction programming.

Part Five:

Unveiling Addiction
For What The Addiction Is

Dr. Angela®

"Addiction, I see past your mask."

13
Addiction Inhabits

Addiction patterns **inhabit** us, they are not us. For us to address these invasive patterns, we must begin to *differentiate ourselves* from these patterns.

The following perspective does not in any way remove responsibility from the client experiencing problem addiction. The client remains responsible for addressing, reducing the power of, even where possible overriding and or rewiring, this:

**invasive
programming.**

I have seen it, I really have, and I suggest my Readers can as well. Consider this view I have developed in working with the persons and the minds of several thousand people over several decades....

ADDICTION IS A <u>PROGRAMMING</u> WE CARRY: A PROGRAMMING TO BE HIGHLY ADDICT-ABLE

Addiction is a program we carry within us. We have inherited this program to be what I describe earlier in this book as highly programmable, highly *addict-able*. Once exposed to an addictive drug (including alcohol) or an addictive nondrug behavior, we are at risk of becoming addicted to it and or to other addictive drugs or behaviors. And, we actually are from the start, already out the gate, even prior to exposure, at risk of becoming addicted: We are wired to become addicted, ideally only in healthy ways, however this is not the case for too many persons.

The neuropathology of addiction tells us addiction is a complex brain disorder, generally a chronic relapsing condition, bringing about lasting brain changes with mental health, and cognitive adaptations and consequences. As described by the U.S. National Institute on Drug Abuse (NIDA), most addictive drugs…

> "target the brain's reward system by flooding the circuit with dopamine … a neurotransmitter present in regions of the brain that regulate movement, emotion, cognition, motivation, and reinforcement of rewarding behaviors. When activating at normal levels, this system rewards our natural behaviors. Overstimulating the system with drugs, however, produces effects which strongly reinforce the behavior of drug use, teaching the person to repeat it."[60]

SAME PROGRAM, RADICALLY DIFFERENT AGENDA

After so many hours, months, and years *in the room* with problem addictions, as well as with the clients these problem addictions *inhabit*, it has become clear to me that the *addiction is a presence in itself, has a logic, a purpose, a matrix/mind of its own.*

I use the phrase *in the room* here as, when working with clients experiencing problem addictions, there are times I have clearly sensed the *presence* of the *addiction within the client – some form of*

---

[60] NIDA, *The science of drug use and addiction: the basics.* 2018. <druguse.gov> < https://www.drugabuse.gov/publications/media-guide/science-drug-use-addiction-basics>

presence, a self perpetuating biochemically and bioelectrically formed and reinforced neural pathway and brain process matrix.

This presence is so very PRESENT that I feel it sees me see it. And then, it feels me work with the client to move this presence outside this client's SELF, at least for a while, while I work with the client who senses this process and works with this concept to find, to *discover*, him or her SELF behind the invader's force field.

We must see and speak to this addiction.

I do not mean to be science fiction-like about this, however there is an invader present: the problem addiction is an invasive program that has worked its way deep into the client. *This is not the healthy life oriented programming to form healthy habits, cycles, addictions to healthy behaviors and patterns. This is something masquerading as the same programming but radically different in its agenda.*

INHABITS US

When I say addiction INHABITS us, I am referring to two levels of this INHABITING:

INHERITED PROGRAMING TO BE ADDICTED TO BASIC NECESSARY BEHAVIORS:

This is the INHABITING programming we carry deep within us, within our genes and then within our neural wiring. This is programming to be addict-able. As I noted earlier, being highly addict-able of course has both convenience and survival value. Whether it be eating when nutrition is scarce and finally available, or moving away from danger such as fire, we best respond relatively automatically.

INHERITED PROGRAMMING TO BECOME
ADDICTED TO NEW BEHAVIORS:

A second level of this INHABITING is programming to take on new patterns, new habits, new cycles of behavior we are not born with. This programming clearly has some convenience and survival value, as we benefit greatly from this capability to *program in new* beneficial behaviors. This is useful, as this way we do not need to relearn every single thing we must do every single time we are confronted with a situation requiring a response from us. For example, automatically stopping at red lights while driving is most definitely beneficial to us. At each red light encounter, we do not need to take the time to relearn the meaning of the light and how to stop the car. (We transfer previous learning to new situations.) We just stop. However, this ease of programmability (ease of pattern acquiring) we have inherited also leaves us open to easily acquiring bad habits, problem patterns, and dangerous addictions.

Addiction INHABITS us because the programming inhabits us: we are programmed to become addicted to patterns. This programming leaves us open to becoming addicted to problem patterns, or problem pattern addictions.

WE MUST CALL
PROBLEM ADDICTION OUT OF THE SHADOWS

This brings me right back to the raison d'être of this book, *GESTALTING ADDICTION.* I have long seen the addict, and I see now that this addict is NOT us, but is *inhabiting us,* and not always to our benefit. My view is that to work with persons who are experiencing problem addictions, we must gestalt the addictions inhabiting these persons—inhabiting all of us for that matter. We must **call these addictions out from behind their masks, out from their cover, out from their disguising themselves AS US.**

***Addiction itself must be identified, addressed, called out of hiding, GESTALTED, told it is to step away from the core of the person, the client, it is INHABITING.

***The person experiencing problem addiction can be helped to sense that he/she is *not* the problem addiction programming. Although we hear the opposite of this so many places, this mixing the individual in with his/her addiction as in, "you are an addict, admit it," this is not exactly the case.

***We can allow clients to differentiate themselves from their addictions, to see themselves as not the addict, but as the person seeking to expel (or at least control) the invasive programming.

***The addiction itself has to be related to, addressed, as an *invader* seeking to sneak in while appearing as someone's own addiction, sickness, or disease, even as part of someone's own SELF.

***The addiction is not our client, or our client's behavior or attitude...

**the addiction is
an invasive program
that is occupying the
client's mind and body.**

NOTE AGAIN:
This perspective does not in any way remove responsibility from the client experiencing problem addiction. The client remains responsible for addressing, reducing the power of, rewiring, even where possible deleting, this...

invasive programming.

The addiction is in the room. We do best to begin to call the addiction out of its hiding within the client. In this sense, we best help the circle of persons facing their addictions *to see and separate themselves, their identities, from the invasive addictions* that have overtaken so many parts of them. (See *Chapters 24, 25, 26.)*

14
Gestalting
The Trojan Horse Camouflaging
The Truth About Addiction

This thing we call *addiction*, whether it is what I call a *problem* addiction (such as an addiction to alcohol or other drugs or behaviors) or what I call a *necessary* addiction (such as one we may develop to be automatically stopping at red traffic lights), is so deeply embedded, so entirely ubiquitous in its presence and reach, that it is a given we simply accept. Indeed we accept many addictions largely without thinking about them.

BEING ADDICT-ABLE

Being *addict-able* is an ever present always active program we are coded, wired, to carry within ourselves. Indeed, this thing we call addiction digs into us so very deeply i*t disguises itself as us.* Oh yes, this thing we call addiction is the ultimate Trojan horse luring us into itself by its very duality, its both life protecting and life threatening sides (frequently disguising themselves as each other).

Ultimately, we are creatures of habit, with very little exception. We do not recognize ourselves as so very habituated and habituate-able. Yet we are so very much so: we are carriers of genetic programming and neural wiring operating and directing our every thought, idea, emotion, and action. [Certainly our programming and wiring interacts with environment to function (to identify, intake, process data, also acquire nourishment, respond to triggers, etc.), yet this programming to be addict-able is wired right into us, as if we are bio-bots.]

GESTALTING ADDICTION
TO KNOW IT

On the pages of this book, I seek to reach beyond my and others' previous discussions and definitions of both these terms, "addiction" and "gestalt." Let's rethink, reformat, our notions of these terms, *addiction* and *gestalt*. Let's step away from holding to narrow and at times confining, even distorting, definitions and applications of these terms, *addiction* and *gestalt*.

In the latter regard, although I do talk about gestalt *therapy* in this book, primarily regarding underpinning concepts behind this therapy,[61] I seek more to get at the ideas behind *any gestalt of anything*, and in the particular case of this book, what I describe as:

the

gestalt of

addiction itself.

TROJAN HORSE
AND OTHER LIFE FORMS

Again, what I am saying here is that there is more to this *gestalting* of *addiction* I am describing, more than directing the performing of gestalt therapy on/with patients, clients, others. I therefore seek to

---

[61] I come to this discussion from a different perspective, with a different goal, looking beyond simply exemplifying or teaching the practice of traditional gestalt therapy, a curriculum I leave to other settings.

gestalt addiction itself, to call addiction out of its hiding within us, within our deepest realms, within our deepest coding to be addicted. This *gestalting* **OF** *addiction* I am doing here is calling out …

…addiction as an opportunistic program within us.

Again…

addiction hides behind us, disguises itself AS us.

Too frequently when there is a problem addiction, this problem programming/patterning merges with us to such an extent that its treatment (in therapy, in doctors' offices, in treatment centers, in hospitals, etc.) feels to some addicted persons like an assault upon them—an assault taking place while they struggle to unravel themselves from this Trojan Horse we call addiction. We feel the struggle, it is real, as if the addiction itself is alive and is fighting back, seeking to stop our realizing its invasive programming is present.

**If we look,
we can see this
monumental tug of war
taking place within us.**

Push pull, tug toward, tug away.

**Here is where it becomes clear that
we are not "our" addictions.
We are not this invader.**

HERE IS THE
DOUBLE BINDING NATURE OF ADDICTION

Revealing the invasion of us by this Trojan Horse, this problem addiction pattern programming, highlighting its *sneaking into our identity* by invading our brain's programming, must be done now. Let's begin by recognizing the following:

1. This problem addiction pattern is in essence a Trojan Horse that has made its way into us by being VIEWED BY US AS US.
2. We are *not* this Trojan Horse, this invader of us, hiding within us by posing as us. We are *not* these problem addictions, we are *not* this problem addiction programming.
3. Here is the double bind that problem addiction patterns pull us into and seek to hold us trapped in: **REJECTING THE PROBLEM ADDICTION CAN FEEL VERY CLOSE TO REJECTING OURSELVES.** So very many persons seeking to weaken or break (or let die) their problem addictions speak these words, "I feel like I am dying."
4. Yet, when working to break a problem addiction, what is dying is the problem addiction pattern and not the person it has inhabited.
5. The double binding problem addiction pattern seeks to hold us in its pattern program by invading even our self definition. We must retrieve who we are from problem addiction patterns. These problem patterns can invade so many levels of us, of who we believe we are, including our identity itself.
6. Glimpsing the release from the double bind is a great gestalt, an insight AHA--the glimpse of the release from not knowing the way out of a trapping situation, the glimpse of the way to open the exit door. This is just a start, yet this AHA insight must take place to *set the release in motion*. This initiates the transformational learning of *gestalting addiction*.
7. Now we must sustain this release to transform ourselves..

15
The Identified Addict

The problem addiction pattern is a highly invasive program, so invasive that the SELF can be drawn into *confusing itself with, mistaking its identity for,* the addiction pattern programming.

IDENTIFYING THE ADDICT AS WHO/WHAT

The more the problem addiction program has invaded the self, the more the self has absorbed the problem addiction pattern/program into its identity. This makes the problem addiction very difficult, at times life and death difficult, to reduce, control, leave, break free of.

The severely addicted individual who has come to feel that she/he is "basically just a lifelong addict" has a life being dominated by problem addiction programming, its tendrils reaching deeply into the identity itself.

Yet, again note, the addict is the addiction programming, not the individual this programming has invaded.

**The addiction is the invasive program
and not the program's host, not us.**

THE TRUTH ABOUT
THE IDENTITY OF THE ADDICT

The identified addict is frequently viewed as the person experiencing the problem addiction to drugs/alcohol or to a non-drug behavior.

YET, LOOK AGAIN:
THE IDENTIFIED ADDICT IS THE
PROBLEM ADDICTION PROGRAM ITSELF.

IP NOT IA

Too frequently, the apparently "addicted person" is called the "identified patient" or IP. Yet, we must not let ourselves confuse this IP label with what I term the "identified addict" or IA, however confused these concepts may be in our thinking. Let's not allow the addiction programming to rule our own perceptions of what and who the addiction actually is. It is the problem addiction *program* that should be the called the identified addict, the IA, not the individual *person*, not the self itself.

IP ← is not the → IA

Certainly, we still want to provide treatment to persons infected by the problem addiction pattern programming. Yet we must draw a distinction between the identity of the IP,[62] the individual patient (or as I term this, the client) and the identity of the invasive problem addiction program which is the actual IA. This distinction is not only fair, it is essential. Problem addiction is a chronic and frequently life damaging and life threatening brain disease, an infection by an insidious opportunistic program. Let us always keep in mind that...

the afflicted individual is not the disease.

---

[62] The very important discussion regarding the incorrect or biased labeling of an individual in a family as the only IP (when other family members may be deflecting their own possible identification/s as persons with IP-like symptoms) is reserved for other publications. See the *INTERNATIONAL COLLECTION ON ADDICTIONS.*

PARALLEL BOUNDARY
CONFUSION

With this inherent confusion that the problem addiction program is designed to generate, with the program's *distortion of the boundaries between the self and the addiction*, it follows that the addicted person is likely to experience *boundary confusion on all levels*. **The problem addiction program seeks to compromise the boundaries between the self and the addiction. Other personal boundaries also experience pressure and then parallel confusion.**

PEOPLE AROUND
ARE DRAWN IN

With the compromising of boundaries within the "addicted person," the compromising of boundaries around that person can also take place. It is not surprising that persons close in to an "addicted individual" are at risk of being sucked into the "addicted person's" patterns, even that person's reality. (Recall the old co-addiction adage, "She went to jump off the Golden Gate Bridge, and his entire life flashed before her eyes.")

When persons around the identified patient or what some will say is the identified addict are engaged in the problem patterns of that "addicted person," all of their boundaries are weakening and blurring. This is almost (if not entirely) a biochemical and energetic process. The problem pattern has not only invaded the one addicted individual, the so called "addict," but frequently also has invaded the persons around that individual, the so called "co-addicts."

The problem pattern program reaches past interpersonal boundaries into others close to the identified patient to lure them into supporting the problem pattern. The profound danger faced by those around a so-called "addicted person" is generally overlooked, not seen or emphasized enough. Not only do co-habiting persons miss seeing some if not all of the boundary transgression dangers they themselves face, others outside may also not see the whole picture. The profound danger faced by those around a so-called "addicted person" is generally overlooked, not seen or emphasized enough.[63]

---

[63] The matter of boundaries is central, even at times life saving, for family members, especially when there are severe addictions present. I refer here to an event a client spoke of during a therapy session as she discussed her husband's severe poly-drug addictions. One morning, she was expected to join her husband on a drive out to an event. She had been avoiding being a passenger when he was driving, as he had been "drugging himself so much lately." This particular morning, she again felt she simply could not join him. When he pressured her, she told him she would only go if she could drive his car. He said no, and grew very angry with her that she was refusing to join him, and even angrier when she begged him not to go, even without her, telling him she felt he was in danger as he'd been "using" so much lately. She even went so far as to throw the car keys out into a field near their house. Her husband simply got his spare key and prepared to leave. He again demanded she join him. She hesitated a moment, almost saying yes. But she again said no and that he should not go either. When she went to take that spare key away as well, he struck her hard and threw her to the ground. Stunned, bruised, cut, and bleeding, when she was finally able to stand up, he was in the car and racing down the driveway. ... Several hours later she received a call telling her he had just been in a serious accident and was being taken to the hospital. As she rushed to the hospital she realized that: had she not objected to joining him, had she not held firm in support of her own boundary, she would have been in that accident with him. In that moment, she realized that she had to form very clear physical, emotional, even energetic boundaries around herself, to pull herself out of his problem addiction pattern for once and for all. What later became more clear to her was this: In her *gestalting addiction* work with me, she realized the presence of the insidious invasive addiction pattern that she had been speaking to while begging her husband not to go on that drive. "Now I see that I was married to my husband, but also to that problem addiction pattern that had invaded him. Not only would my husband not let go of me, his addiction also would not let me go."

WE JUST DO NOT SEE
THE ADDICTION PROGRAM
AT WORK

The addiction programming seeks to have its disguise continue. The addiction program seeks to have the addicted person and others around him/her identify the addicted person as the identified addict (IA) so as not to recognize the invading addiction program's presence.

Again, the Trojan Horse of problem addiction is so invasive, and so stealth in its invasiveness, that we do not fully see what is being invaded (ourselves), nor that an invasion has taken, is taking, place. It is time to see this, to call, to gestalt, problem addiction programming out of the shadows. Here is where we can take a real gestalt, the *gestalting of addiction*, to the invading addiction program, to the Trojan Horse itself.

16
On
Deleting
This Thing
We Call Addiction

It is such a long way home, back to me.
Will anyone ever live there again?

(Anonymous Group Therapy Participant)

Problem addiction pattern programming is not going away. It may dress itself up differently, or change our minds about its nature. Yet, this problem programming is here, and likely here to stay. Problem addiction programming may not ever be entirely deleted. It may however be reset, refocused, rewired, overridden.

Hello addiction program, we know you. At least we think we know you. We have been living with you and or around you for so very long now. Indeed, it is in *our* nature to form *your* addictions, even in our genetic coding to do so.

ADDICTION IS PART OF US

So the addiction programming is part of us, within and all around us, and yes, so far as we know, "it" (this "problem") is not going to go entirely away. But, what is this "it" that is not going away? What is this "it" we are looking at here? Can we see this "it"? Can we define this "it"? Can we know this "it"? Can we talk to this "it" as "it" lurks within us? I say yes: we can gestalt this "it," this addiction (as in *Chapter 24*). We can even have this "it," this addiction program, gestalt itself (as in *Chapter 25*).

Can we come face to face with this IT? Can we call this IT out of the recesses of ourselves? I say YES.

PROBLEM ADDICTION PROGRAMMING:
ARE YOU OUT THERE?
ARE YOU IN HERE?
CAN I TALK TO YOU?
CAN I SEE YOU?
YES.

AM I YOU?
ARE YOU ME?
NO.

Your problem addiction program, its problem addiction pattern, is not you; however, unraveling your addiction from yourself is a challenge for so many reasons. Although we are not our biological bodies, we identify with our biological bodies so very much that untying an addiction from within our bodies and brains feels like cutting out a piece of ourselves.

SURVIVAL REQUIRES SOME PROGRAMMING

We are biological life forms, animals, programmed for what were once likely survival oriented reasons to become addicted to yes, necessary, yes, even survival oriented behaviors. We have maintained this innate capability to addict to necessary behaviors for generations, for long phases of our evolution or development, most likely, if I might suggest this, even since our (design and) genesis. (I leave it to Readers of this book to interpret genesis and design according to their own preferences and beliefs.)

If we look at this remarkable programming phenomenon, at this great convenience, we perhaps should be grateful that our species has survived thus far here on this planet Earth. And we should perhaps thank our lucky stars that we are programmed to become addicted to necessary, even survival oriented, behaviors. Again…

**WE ARE
HIGHLY PROGRAMMABLE LIFE FORMS,
BEINGS GENETICALLY CODED
TO BE RECEPTIVE TO PROGRAMMING
THAT ALLOWS US
TO BECOME "ADDICTED" TO BEHAVIORS
WE NEED TO HAVE
FUNCTION AUTOMATICALLY
TO ALLOW US
TO SURVIVE.**

This program-ability is a great success for our species, as for many others: we are still here, walking this planet. We even know (consciously in some ways, and sub- and un- consciously for the most part) how to program ourselves to function in this modern world, to stop automatically at those red traffic lights, etc.

**PROBLEM
PROGRAMMING**

Such a wonderful convenience is this deeply embedded, virtually essential to survival, self programming function we carry.

YET WE ARE STARTING TO SEE THAT SOMETHING IS NOT WORKING WELL.

Deep within ourselves, where we carry this capability to program ourselves, we find this necessary program-ability function of ours is running far afield, seemingly out of control. **Or, and I dare also ask this: Is the addiction pattern program actually *in* control, seeking ever greater control over its hosts—over us?**

(And, I do at times also ask this additional question: Might this programming actually also include programming to **appear** to be healthy programming running awry while quietly pressing its **invasion ever deeper** into our minds and bodies? I reserve this for another discussion.[64])

And, when this running awry happens, we can almost obediently grow quite detrimentally, even quite dangerously, addicted to using drugs/alcohol, substances, and to other dangerous behaviors more in the nondrug (non-substance) arenas. These drug and nondrug (so called behavioral) addictions are perilously prevalent these days, and ongoing. It seems we, even with all our well intentioned science and religion and the essential self help and peer practices, have of course neither backed this problem away nor fully understood what this problem is.

---

[64] See books in the *CONSCIOUSNESS AND SURVIVAL SERIES* such as *UNVEILING THE HIDDEN INSTINCT* and also *OVERRIDING THE EXTINCTION SCENARIO*. Refer to recommended reading list at the end of this present book, *GESTALTING ADDICTION*.

Deep within the recesses of our minds, and the biological brains that carry our minds, we find microscopic, even submicroscopic, processes enacting themselves according to our programming. While in several other books I discuss consciousness and what consciousness is or might be,[65] here I want to look at the brain's programming for what it is and for what it does to us.

Of course, as the brain IS US (or a key part of us and our consciousness) according to most scientists, then this book does address the consciousness. (Indeed, I do share my *Going Conscious Processes* in *Part Six* of this book, with our consciousness as a key factor.)

This being said, be on the lookout for the enslavement of the person, or of that person's brain, or of that person's mind, or of that person's consciousness – to problem addiction itself.

Biochemical and bioelectric, and other forms of messages less known to us, race through our brains, spilling among our cells, neural pathways, and synapses, directing our choices, actions, feelings, and all that relates to these. It is there, at the most invisible micro level, that our biologies decide whether we will grow addicted and to what we will grow addicted, and what the effects of our addictions will be.

So how free are we, one might want to ask here. Are we free enough to: (a) choose to or not to be addicted; and to (b) choose what to or not to be addicted to? Not entirely, not entirely free that is. (Our free will itself can be invaded, usurped, controlled by problem addiction programming.)

---

[65] See books listed in previous footnote.

HERE WE ARE, CONSCIOUSNESS

So here we are again, face to face with what some will tell us is indeed the consciousness, or at least what the *self* thinks is its own consciousness.[66]

Yes we are, to some extent, *what* our biological brains tell us we are, *who* our brains tell us we are. And we may live there, in that biological brain, right down in there at the submicroscopic level. Or we may have the option to override what takes place under the radar, deep down in there. We may have the option to override invasive programming that can work on this level where our *aware* consciousness does not readily go.[67]

Yet we are not simply what we find there. The persona, the will, the being, whatever its source, is more than a cellular or electro-biochemical thing. And it is more than a collection of these things. The whole is greater than the sum of its parts. So are we.

WE CAN GESTALT THE ADDICTIONS

We are, whatever we are, more than simply a biological process. And these selves we have, these selves that can run into challenges and problems in living, can speak to us.

When a problem addiction pattern overtakes us, takes control of our *selves*, we can talk to our *selves* and also to the addictions dominating them (us). Yes, we can.

---

[66] See again, *UNVEILING THE HIDDEN INSTINCT* listed in the recommended reading at the end of this book.
[67] Again, refer to the books, *UNVEILING THE HIDDEN INSTINCT* and also *OVERRIDING THE EXTINCION SCENARIO, Part One.*

As I further explain in *Part Six*, we can call what is influencing us, operating us, driving us, out of the shadows. We can ***gestalt the problem addiction pattern program*** that drives us. We can differentiate ourselves from these patterns to find our SELVES in there, behind these patterns of addiction, to allow us to unveil our SELVES to ourselves.

Part Six:

Unveiling, Gestalting, and Confronting The Addiction In Therapy

Dr. Angela®

"Addiction, I see you now.
Think you can fool me? Control me? Kill me?
NO, I won't let that happen."

17
About Part Six:
On Gestalting
The Paradox of Addiction

Part Six of this book offers a brief look at some of my work utilizing the perspectives and concepts I have presented in the previous chapters. While it would take one of my multiday workshops or several large volumes to detail in full my GESTALTING ADDICTIONS AND LIFE ISSUES practices and procedures, here I highlight some of the basics of my process of gestalting addiction in therapy and treatment settings.

Note that these are not lessons in basic gestalt therapy exercises and processes, as there is a great deal of literature available in that area. Rather, this is what I have developed to address problem addiction, the concepts and processes of GESTALTING the ADDICTION, and then of having the ADDICTION GESTALT itself.

As this process of **gestalting addiction** unfolds, the double binding paradox of addiction itself grows ever more explicit. This becomes apparent as the following chapters proceed.

Noting (several times along the way) to clients and other participants in this process: what paradox is; what the paradox of addiction is; what a double bind is; how this paradoxical double bind is experienced, felt, responded to – develops awareness of the sensation, situation, and paradox of addiction programming and how to address this.

THE VALUABLE PARADOXICAL DOUBLE BIND

Underscoring this *GESTALTING ADDICTIONS AND OTHER LIFE ISSUES* work I have developed over the years is the matter of the *paradoxical double bind,* and how we find this paradoxical double bind in life in general, as well as in problem addiction, and in other mental, physical, spiritual, and societal health and well being arenas.

To wit, I speak of: what stages and patterns of our emotions, behaviors, and addictions we can identify and gain more conscious engagement in and control of; the ongoing, even inherent, paradoxical nature of addiction; how this paradoxical nature and its double bind can be gestalted; and how problem addiction itself can be called further out of hiding, out from the inner recesses of our sub- and un- consciousnesses so that we may be able to gain more conscious control over this problem addiction patterning itself.

SEEING THE INVASIVE ADDICTION PROGRAMMING

What is ever more clear here is that the opportunistic invasive problem addiction programming runs *counter to the goals of its host—of US.* Of course this is obviously a meta level paradox, yet one we must never let ourselves overlook. The problem addiction requires its host to live, yet the problem addiction program will confuse its host, disguise itself *as its host,* control its host, even in the extreme kill its host — US -- in order for itself, the problem program, to "survive." (This sounds sadly similar to a cancer or other disease living on or in its host, yet draining even killing its host.)[68]

---

[68] How also sadly similar this phenomenon is to what humans may be doing to the Earth's biosphere, using it of course to survive yet draining

198

PROGRAMMING OF		PROGRAMMING OF
ORGANISM	versus	PROBLEM ADDICTION
survival of organism:		survival of problem addiction:
the organism's		the problem addiction's
programming to survive		programming to survive

The paradox is clear. On the one hand, generally speaking, a living organism seeks to survive, is wired, programmed to survive, as most instincts suggest.[69] On the other hand, the problem addiction programming is designed (or has designed itself) to have the problem addiction survive. This drive of the problem addiction runs counter to the drive of its host organism, an organism normally programmed to survive (for example, to eat, sleep, reproduce, respond to threats to safety with fight or flight reflexes, etc.).

For a healthy organism to follow the directive of a problem addiction is not only counter intuitive and counterproductive, it is counter survival. And yet both systems' (the organism's and the problem addiction's) programmings operate in the same body — OURS. Furthermore, the organism's survival programming and the problem addiction's survival programming utilize many of the

---

it, potentially killing it, while so doing. Refer to the books where I further develop this matter: OVERRIDING THE EXTINCTION SCENARIO, Part One and Part Two, and UNVEILING THE HIDDEN INSTINCT.

[69] There is the matter of individual survival plus the population or species survival. I do not address this matter in this book. Some theorists juxtapose the individual and its species. However, I take a different view. See OVERRIDING THE EXTINCTION SCENARIO for my perspective on this.

same brain mechanisms to operate, such as the brain's reward pathway/s, attention functions, decision making functions, etc.[70]

IN THE FOLLOWING CHAPTERS:
THE GOING CONSCIOUS PROCESS
IN GESTALTING ADDICTION

In the following chapters, I offer a discussion of the thinking and processes I share with individual and group therapy clients and workshop participants as they move into *going ever more conscious* and GESTALTING (their) ADDICTIONS. The following chapters simply highlight a few of the interwoven informational and experiential processes I have designed and are not intended to be a full description of these. The following chapters move through concepts and processes rather fluidly, in the general flow of their actual presentation to clients and workshop participants. Of course, a great deal of direct dialog and interaction with clients regarding these concepts are for the most part not included here in this overview of these *Going Conscious* and *Gestalting Addiction Processes.*

Again note, these chapters are not a lesson in conducting gestalt therapy. Rather, these chapters describe my general teaching and processes of moving into *heightening awareness* and *gestalting addiction*. I engage in sharing these concepts and experiential activities with clients in the general order of the following *Part Six* chapters. These chapters are also portions of the trainings I provide psychotherapists, clinicians, and others working in this arena:

---

[70] I offer an in depth look at various brain functions affected by addiction in the volume on psychobiology of addiction included in the four volume series, the *INTERNATIONAL COLLECTION ON ADDICTIONS.*

- Seeing the Power of Paradox (*Chapter 18*)
- Seeing the Four Basic (and Repeatable) Stages of Our Journey
  (*Chapter 19*)
- Mapping the Four Basic Stages of Our Journey (*Chapter 20*)
- Recognizing and Facing Ingrained Problem Pattern Addiction
  (*Chapter 21*)
- Undrugging the Feelings (*Chapter 22*)
- The Going Conscious Process (*Chapter 23*)
- Gestalting Addiction (*Chapter 24*)
- Addiction Gestalting Itself (*Chapter 25*)
- Navigating the Emotional Terrain in Gestalting Addiction
  (*Chapter 26*)

18
Seeing
The Power of Paradox

Paradox and the double bind it wears can be a metaphorical gold mine in psychotherapy, as here is a source of energy that can be freed for insight, elevation, and change:

PARADOX

The energy held, caught, even trapped, in this paradox, this bind, can be guided to a positive release, gestalted to a new level of understanding, awareness, and action.

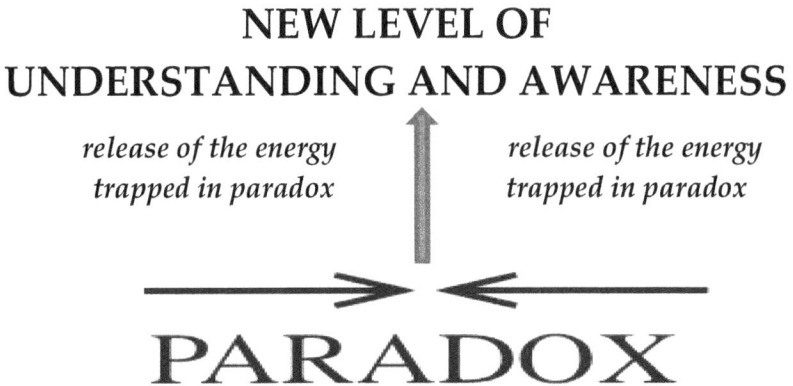

NEW LEVEL OF
UNDERSTANDING AND AWARENESS

release of the energy   *release of the energy*
trapped in paradox   *trapped in paradox*

PARADOX

DOUBLE BINDING PARADOX

As noted in earlier chapters, a double bind is a situation in which a person is faced with a choice between two or more undesirable courses of action, and or two or more irreconcilable requirements.[71]

Persons caught in problem pattern addiction are experiencing the double bind of addiction itself:
        (1) the lose if I use scenario versus
        (2) the lose if I don't use scenario.
The pressure to exit this paradox can be brought on by events and situations the addicted person experiences, such a medical, legal, economic, family, or other crisis calling for the halting of the problem addiction behavior.

However, this form of externally initiated crisis propelled release is frequently not an actual emotional, cognitive, and or spiritual release, as it tends not to carry with it the AHA insight that truly can catalyze profound release – that is, if the insight itself is sustained, elevated. (See *Chapters 4 and 24*.)

---

[71] Recall the earlier quotes of and references to the views of Gregory Bateson in this area, such as: "...My debt to A.A. will be evident throughout—also...my respect for its co-founders, Bill W. and Dr. Bob. ... [Also note] the famous *Serenity Prayer*: 'God grant us the serenity to accept the things we cannot change, courage to change the things we can, and wisdom to know the difference.' **If double binds cause anguish and despair... then it follows, conversely, that for healing these wounds ... some converse of the double bind will be appropriate**. The [bond of the] double bind leads to ... [the] despair [that is saying], 'There are no alternatives.' ... The *Serenity Prayer* **explicitly frees** the worshipper from these maddening bonds." [Gregory Bateson, *The Cybernetics of "Self": A Theory of Alcoholism*. Cited earlier.]

Crisis can indeed force an exit from a paradox. Note however that forced exit from paradox may or may not encourage a lasting change, elevation, in behavior. (See *Chapter 19*.)

THE POWER IN JUXTAPOSITION

Think of the famous *liar's paradox: Everything I say is a lie*. Therefore, this statement itself is a lie, yet it proves itself true by being the lie that it says it is. A paradox is a self (or other) contradictory statement, communication, or situation, frequently causing not only confusion but psychological distress.[72]

Yet, paradox can be immensely useful. One of the best examples of powerful use of paradox is when it is used as a literary device where "paradox is the juxtaposition of a set of seemingly contradictory concepts that **reveal a hidden and/or unexpected truth**."[73]

**Juxtaposition is the process of
clarifying and pressing
the paradox,**

---

[72] Gregory Bateson's Double Bind Theory (and other early proponents' theories of family and family systems' effects on mental health) proposed that symptoms of schizophrenia are an expression of double bind-like communication in the family environment. While critics of this theory have correctly noted that there are most definitely other (and even biologically-based) "causes" of schizophrenia, and that there have been no research data clearly linking schizophrenic symptomatology to such double bind communications, none have detracted from the general notion that double binding communication can cause significant psychological distress. Nor has the powerful model of the double bind itself, and its utility in numerous arenas, been denied.

[73] Literary Devices, Terms, Elements,
http://www.literarydevices.com/paradox/

the parameters of its double bind.

In this juxtaposition, a truth can be revealed.

ON ENCOURAGING RELEASE

In the context of psychotherapy, what I call the *therapeutic juxtaposition* can highlight for clients the factors and forces forming their double binds. *Pressing this juxtaposition* (see *Chapters 21, 22, 23, 24*) can ...

catalyze the energetic release from the double bind.

I have come to describe *encouraging* this release, when this encouraging is guiding a powerful shift and movement in, freeing of, energy, as *catalyzing* this release. Keep in mind that catalyzing is a serious responsibility. This infers that the guide, the psychotherapist, if skilled enough, can indeed guide the client toward this release, *and can then guide (immediately and over time) the client in sustaining positive effects of this release.*

Note that the release itself is up to the client, not the therapist. Such a shift or release can never be imposed upon a client or demanded of a client. This simply does not work as the client must choose this release for him or her self, internally, (including at the moment just before the release). The psychotherapist does best to inform the client of this at all points along the way.

WE ALL KNOW PARADOX

Paradox is part of life and living. The more we *sensitize ourselves to minor and major paradox sensation*s, the more aware we are of the energy held in paradox. This is highly valuable energy that, if released with awareness, can be used to propel, to catalyze, emotional and behavioral (even cognitive) shifting and change.

We all know paradox in some way. **If you are tuning into the sensations of your own minor and major paradoxes, you will learn to notice the trapped and stuck energies of stress, confusion, despair, even of the addiction itself**.

Of course, we may not be constantly if ever thinking directly of paradox. Neither the term nor the experience of paradox may always be explicitly on our minds. Yet paradox is waiting in the wings, there on the edges of our awareness, our aware consciousness, when not revealing itself, when not appearing front and center in our lives.

Those experiencing problem addictions to alcohol/drugs and other addictive behaviors such as gambling, gaming, spending, hoarding, etc. know the paradox of: (1) engaging in the addicted behavior versus (2) refraining from engaging and experiencing the withdrawals, longings, cravings, and other "suffering" the refraining brings. Problem addiction brings with it its very own lose-lose sensation of double binding paradox.

Life presents so many experiences of difficult choices. Frequently, there appear to be no right or best, or perhaps even no workable, answers, no way out of a situation or condition. The experience of paradox is frequently with us. If we are keenly aware, we see paradox is always there, as there is always some level of paradox holding energy trapped or holding energy for us to see and release.

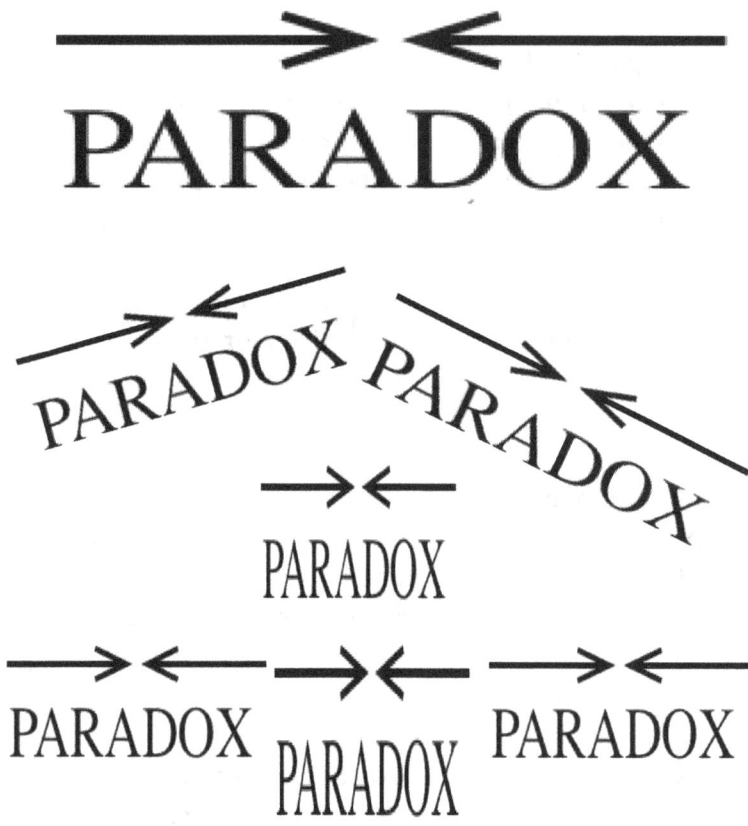

PARADOX

PARADOX PARADOX

PARADOX

PARADOX PARADOX PARADOX

PARADOX

EXTERNALLY-DRIVEN (FORCED?) EXIT FROM PARADOX

Life can bring important events stimulating, propelling, some form of release from paradox or at least from a *harmful holding pattern*. In many instances, while these events are not the potent AHAs, the insight driven releases *gestalting addiction* seeks, these events are challenges, emergencies, crises, that appear to demand or force at least a temporary move out of the harmful situation. As noted earlier, persons experiencing problem pattern addictions may be suddenly faced with pressures (such as those from family, or health emergencies, or legal demands, or other matters) demanding that action be taken, that something be done to address the problem addiction pattern. Such demands and events may indeed save lives.

THE AHA INSIGHT DRIVEN
RELEASE FROM PARADOX

In the context of this *Gestalting Addiction Process*, *the juxtaposition and highlighting of double binding factors* can *catalyze a profound shift* (a brief insight related or lasting elevation related shift) *out of, or release from, the trap of addiction, the double binding lose-lose seeming no way out paradox.* Here is where the promotion of the AHA itself can be guided to bring the client to release him or herself (for a moment or for longer) from the paradoxical condition of addiction. (See *Chapters 23* and *24.)*

The potency of this AHA/release can build via repeating experiences. Indeed this release may require repeat experiences, regular returns to this process of:
  (1) awareness of paradox;
  (2) building of paradox via juxtaposition; and,
  (3) release from paradox…
…as the invasive addiction programming is programmed to take the addicted person back into its domain at every opportunity it detects.

Now, along with release being catalyzed, the AHA of this release being experienced, be aware that options present themselves. Almost concurrently with the AHA release from the double binding paradox, is the question regarding whether to do something to preserve this release, to stay out of the cycle or pattern of the problem addiction, or to not do more to stay with this release. (See the star at the fork in the diagram on below.)

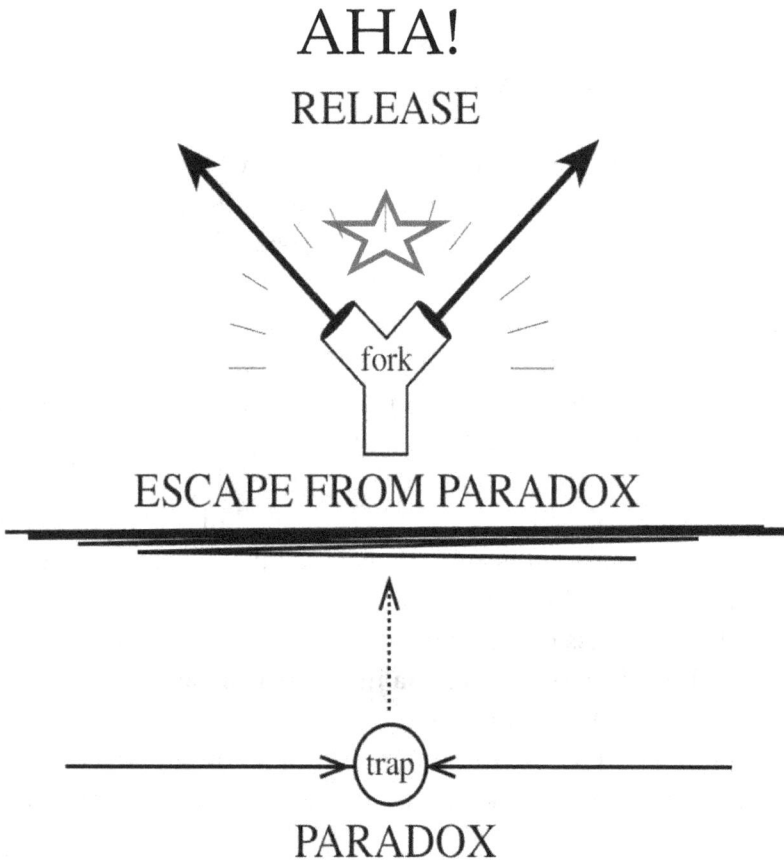

AHA!

RELEASE

fork

ESCAPE FROM PARADOX

trap

PARADOX

Options along the way, as all through life, will present themselves. Understanding what I describe to my clients as being the *emotional terrain*, what stage/s we are in, what the various energies feel like, what the patterns are, can help us identify, become very aware of, and work with, the energy of ourselves and our situations. Let's look more closely at what this means in the following chapter where I offer four basic stages to be aware of and alert to as we begin to gain ever more awareness of our processes and options.

19
Seeing
The Four Basic (and Repeatable) Stages
Of Our Journey

Life is a journey through space and time, heart and mind, self and soul. If we are paying attention, we can see the various passages, phases, stages we move through, sometimes return to, sometimes repeat over and over, sometimes get stalled or trapped in, sometimes learn from and reach higher states of understanding and awareness as a result. Ideally, it is this last option, learning from and reaching higher states of understanding and awareness, that we experience most often. Here is where sensitizing to one's *emotional terrain* is essential.

STAGES OF ONE'S PERSONAL JOURNEY

By stages here I am not referring to conventional stages such as stages of life. Here I am referring to *stages of one's personal journey*. These stages I describe in this chapter are like building blocks, pieces of a journey. We have available to us (whether or not we select or want these) many repeats, re-livings, and redo's of each of these stages, and many versions of each of these stages. As I help clients recognize these stages, I explain that:

I define these stages of one's journey as four basic stages, although each of you will have your own variations of each stage and of each time you experience a stage. What is key here is learning to become ever more aware of the stage or stages you are experiencing.

Ideally, you can learn to recognize, use the energy of, move through, and be consciously aware of your stages -- and of your movement into, through, and beyond each stage. You may even begin to consciously **navigate your own progression** *through the stages of your journey. (See Chapter 20 on mapping these stages of your journey. See also the book where I more fully detail this navigation: NAVIGATING LIFE'S STUFF: SEEING MEANING IN OUR PROCESSES AND PATTERNS.)*

As you learn more about the problem addiction patterning, you may also detect the presence of that patterning in holding you in, or pulling you (back) into, a particular stage (such as struggle or paradox for example).

IMPORTANCE OF RECOGNIZING STAGES

It helps to recognize the stages we are in and or moving through. It is quite valuable to sense the feeling of, or energy present in, each particular stage, to get to know what I call the **emotional terrain** of a particular stage we are experiencing – even the feeling of one's *varying energy patterns during a particular stage.* By energy here, I refer to something other than metabolism or voltage, rather energy in terms of one's overall sense of the mix of— overall pattern of — one's emotional, physical, and other sensations.

Once we are aware of:

> **(a) the general nature of each basic stage;**
> **(b) the particular pattern present in, signaling, each stage;**
> **(c) the stages and places where energy can be trapped; and,**
> **(d) where we can move and use that energy**
> > **to help ourselves...**

...then we can begin to master the stages of and patterns in our lives.

THE FOUR BASIC STAGES

I have distilled these phases, stages, down to four very basic and repeatable stages or patterns:

1) **struggle**
2) **paradox**
3) **insight**
4) **elevation**

Again note that we may move through such stages many times in our lives, indeed even many times a year, month, week, day, or hour.

DEVELOPING
AWARENESS OF STAGES WE ARE IN

Many clients I have guided in individual and group psychotherapy processes have learned to ever more consciously see themselves moving through, in and out of, these stages, to even map the course of their lives according to the varying stages they have found themselves undergoing. (See the next chapter, *Chapter 20*, on consciously mapping the stages of and patterns within our journeys.)

Clients come to understand what they are doing when remaining in a stage that feels problematic, such as do most struggle and paradox stages. Many clients learn not only to recognize themselves in these stages, but to feel, sense, the energy of each particular stage, sometimes energy stuck in a stage, sometimes energy moving freely in personal growth and change processing.

We may move through these stages, one by one, in any particular order. Most likely, we return to each of these stages again (and again and again) in our lives. Of course, we can find ourselves staying in one stage (such as struggle) for quite a while.*** Being ever more aware of the feeling of each stage, and of the energy pattern of each stage, can be quite valuable.

BEFORE PROCEEDING***

Before proceeding to describe each of the four stages or *patternings,* let me say this regarding struggle. In this book discussing *gestalting addiction,* I use the term, *struggle,* to describe a stage in the journey of one's life. I also use this term, and refer to these four basic stages of one's journey, in my work with persons experiencing conditions and situations other than addiction such as mental "blocks," emotional crises, major life changes, aging issues, trauma, shock and grief, death and dying. This is in no way meant to detract from, or disrespect, the serious struggles being experienced by so many people at home and around the world facing hunger, homelessness, war, poverty, disease, persecution, and other devastating, even horrific, circumstances. The pain and devastation these persons are experiencing is severe. My colleagues and I always keep this in mind in our work with clients suffering from problem addictions. We also keep in mind that serious problem addiction can also be severely demoralizing, damaging, devastating, and life threatening.

FOUR BASIC STAGES / PATTERNS
AND THEIR DIAGRAMS

To begin with, I offer clients these simple diagrams (on the following pages) to signify each of the four basic stages or patternings we experience. Each of these stages exhibits its own particular and general energy pattern. If we look closely, we know these energy patterns. This simple introduction to these basic stages of one's life journey allows this material to be readily introduced and very soon applied by clients and others who are looking at their emotional and behavioral "problems," perceptions, sensations, and patterns.

STAGE 1:
STRUGGLE

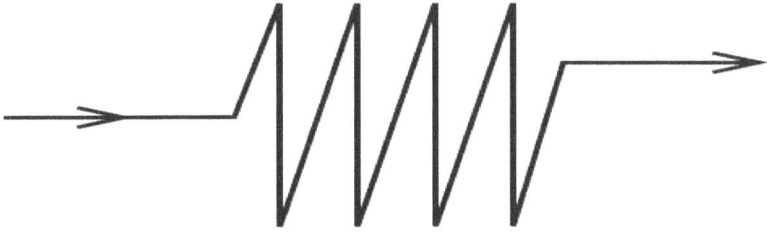

STRUGGLE

Most people are familiar with struggle. Whether minor or major struggles, stages of struggle do come along in life. A particular struggle may appear to take its own form and feel different from another struggle. For example, simply finding a particular location in a city you've never before been to may be a struggle for some people, while fighting to survive is a struggle of an entirely different magnitude.

Whatever the magnitude and category of the struggle stage being experienced, struggles share parallel patterns. The energy is rising and falling, ebbing and flowing, building and dissipating, pushing and pulling -- forces or energies are all working against the person's own stability, and or against the struggle's own resolution. I refer to *resolution* here, as during a struggle, resolution of that struggle is often (although not always) desired. (Yes, there are many times addiction patterns feed on and even reinforce struggle patterns.)

Struggle is struggle. We know what struggle feels like, a sort of back and forth, up and down, energy ebbing and flowing, vying for a stability that it does not reach while struggling. Quite frequently, the sensation of being in the struggle stage includes a sense of being trapped in struggle. At some point, the trap becomes the paradox.

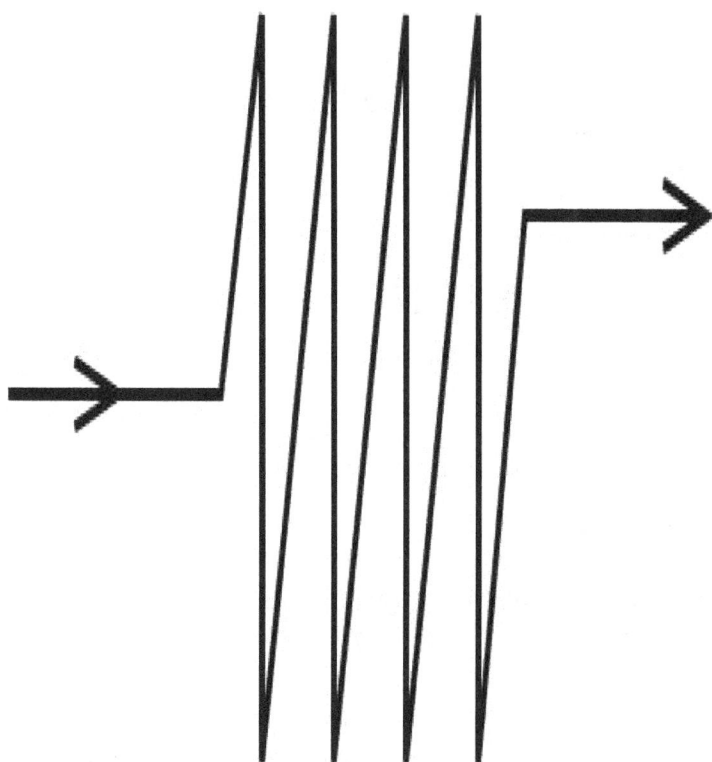

STRUGGLE

STAGE 2:
PARADOX

The discussion of paradox in the previous chapter may define paradox and its double bind experience, however few words can ever fully portray the sensations of being caught, *trapped,* in a double bind. When this is the double bind of problem addiction (the no way out, wrong-wrong, no solution-no solution, lose-lose, pain-pain, sensation with its confusion and frustration, etc.) the Paradox pattern and its sensations can build and build.

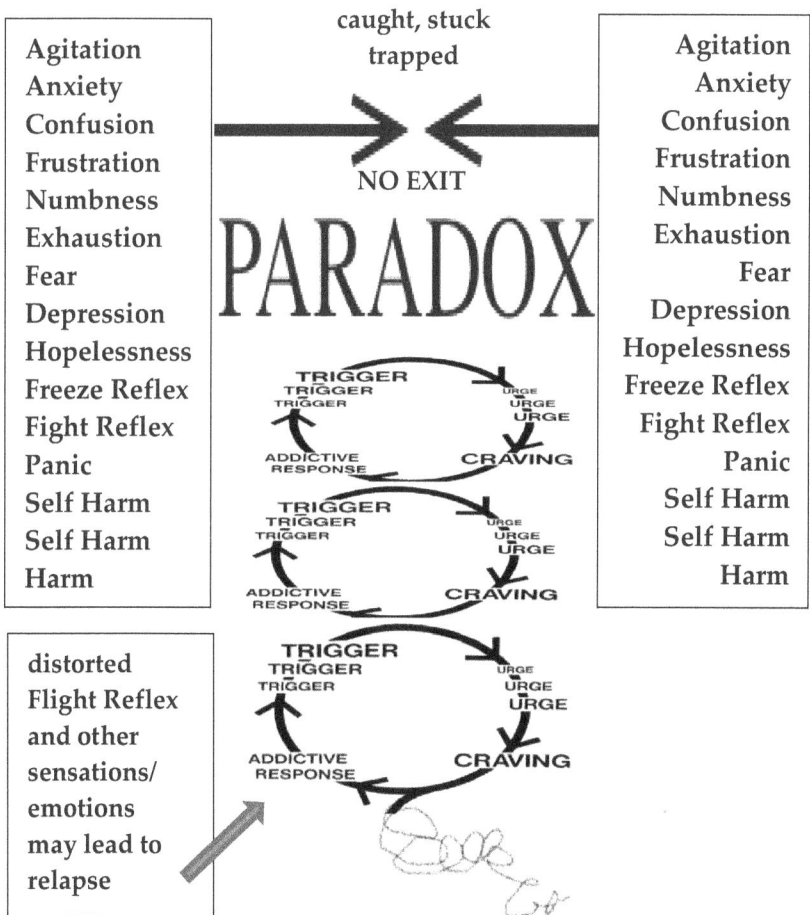

	caught, stuck trapped	
Agitation		Agitation
Anxiety		Anxiety
Confusion	NO EXIT	Confusion
Frustration		Frustration
Numbness		Numbness
Exhaustion	PARADOX	Exhaustion
Fear		Fear
Depression		Depression
Hopelessness		Hopelessness
Freeze Reflex		Freeze Reflex
Fight Reflex		Fight Reflex
Panic		Panic
Self Harm		Self Harm
Self Harm		Self Harm
Harm		Harm

TRIGGER TRIGGER TRIGGER → URGE URGE URGE → CRAVING → ADDICTIVE RESPONSE

distorted Flight Reflex and other sensations/ emotions may lead to relapse

Being caught, seemingly trapped, in the paradoxical pattern of problem addiction, is being caught in that programmed-in cycle, the programmed-in problem addicted brain response. This brain response is the INFECTED GESTALT processing by the problem pattern addiction at work as it controls perceived options, attitudes, responses, actions. (Refer to *Chapter 2* and *Chapter 8*, for example.) The INFECTED gestalt processing is the INFECTED form completion (infected perception) taking the individual right back into the problem pattern (cycle), holding the addicted person in the stage of paradox, in this case, the paradox of addiction. This paradox stage can be pulled, by the addiction programming, right into the problem addiction pattern. And at the same time, the problem pattern can be pulled right into the paradox stage:

A	B
experience of paradox represents part of, pieces of, the whole picture or situation	problem addiction pattern processes and performs INFECTED gestalt to "complete" this picture or situation to its advantage which is to continue the pattern addiction (cycle)

Eventually, the problem addiction program manages to instate the trap and the sensations of paradox right into its problem system. Again, we see the problem addiction pattern usurping whatever it can of the brain/mind's perceptions, experiences, and responses — and subsuming, hijacking, the trapping paradox stage for its own purposes (such as its hosts'—OUR—relapses for the illusion of temporary relief from the trap).

INSIGHT

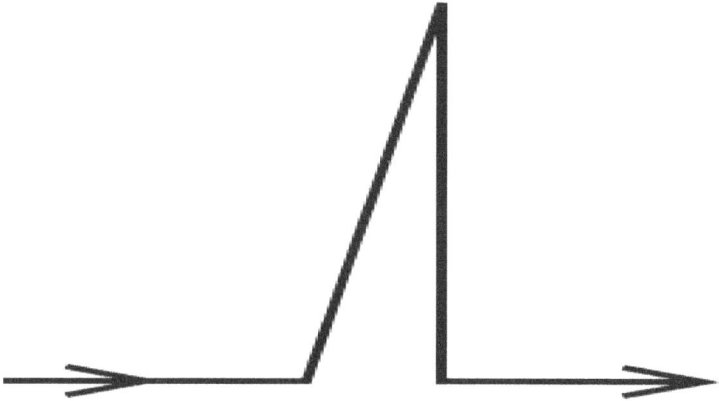

The opportunity to gain a new perspective, to have a glimpse of another option, as well as a sense of a way out of the trap, out the paradoxical double bind of the problem pattern, is available. Such a glimpse, an insight AHA, a moment of seeing beyond the paradox where the person has been trapped or stuck or stalled, is a valuable moment, however brief it may or may not be. (Refer to *Chapters 4* and *24*.)

I say *brief* here, as the insight itself is not necessarily lasting. All too often, the person caught in a problem addiction pattern catches a too brief and too short lived glimpse of the possibility of another option, a way out of the paradoxical trap, the cycle of the problem addiction. Yet, maintaining this insight, holding on to it to rise out and then remain out of the double bind of addiction, involves more. And there can be more. Once insight is sustained, it becomes an actual elevation, for many an elevation of the person's spirit.

INSIGHT

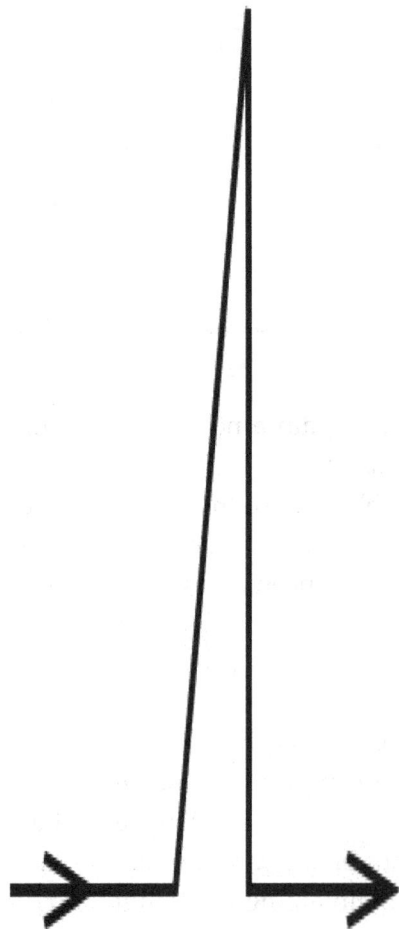

STAGE 4:
ELEVATION

SPIRITUAL
ELEVATION

When an insight is sustained, this insight itself becomes an elevation. This is both an *elevation out of the paradox*, out of the double bind of the addiction pattern, and *an elevation of the awareness, even of the self or spirit or soul* (depending on how the individual labels and perceives these terms). Each of us will define this experience according to how this uplifting shift in perception, emotion, cognition, and resulting behavior feels. For those with a spiritual or religious background, this elevation can be defined according to a chosen belief system. For those without a chosen spiritual or religious belief system, this experience is still an elevation of the self out of the trapping paradox, double bind, of the addiction pattern. The awareness is moved, shifted, out of other stages that have been holding back, resisting, this *transformative shift*. (See *Chapter 4*.)

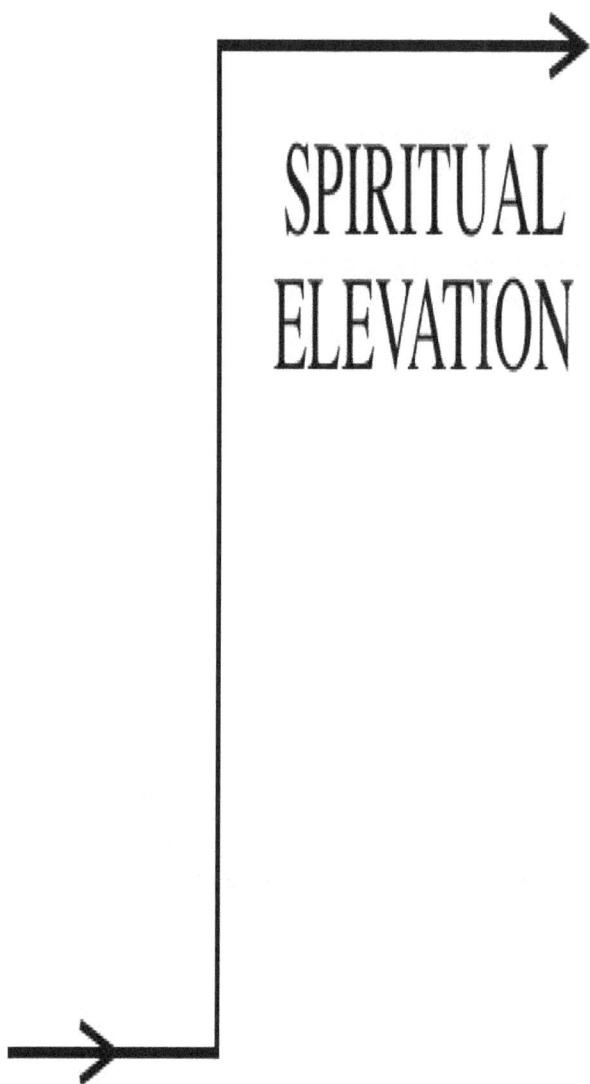

SPIRITUAL
ELEVATION

THE JOURNEY OF THE FOUR STAGES / PATTERNS

Again, sensitizing to one's *emotional terrain* is essential.

Of course, the journey through the four stages defined in this chapter is not one single and direct progression moving just once and always sequentially from *Stage 1: Struggle* to *Stage 2: Paradox* to *Stage 3: Insight* to *Stage 4: Spiritual Elevation* (as in this first illustration immediately below):

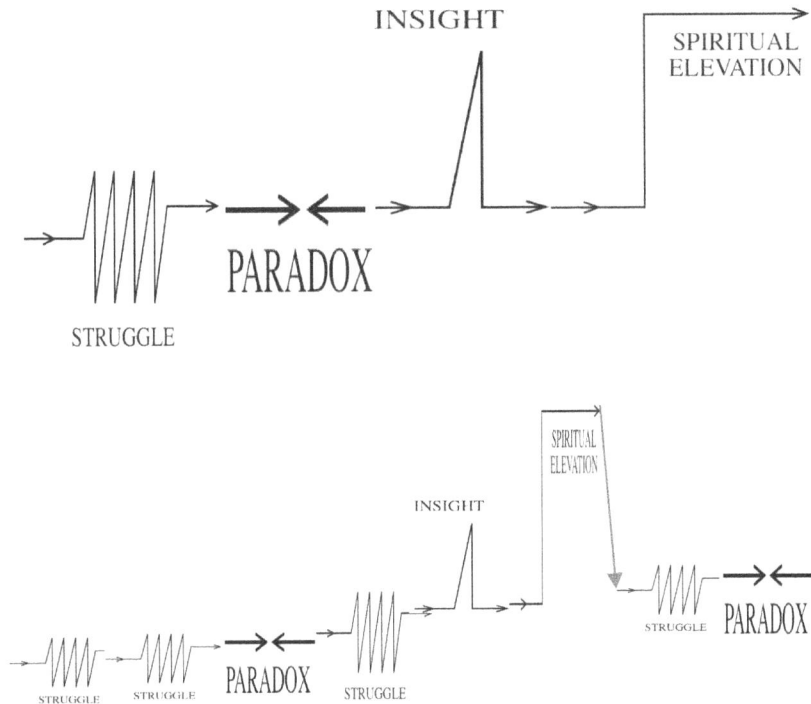

Rather, we repeat stages, move back and forth through and among stages, even reach insight and elevations and then repeat struggles and or paradoxes (as in the lower illustration immediately above). We also can move into new levels of each of these four stages. The next chapter moves us into mapping our journeys from the perspective of these four basic stages.

20
Mapping The Four Basic Stages/Patterns
Of Our Journey

We tend to use geography to tell ourselves where we are. We know the country, state, city, latitude, longitude, and so on. However, there is more to knowing where we are than simply locating ourselves geographically.

GOING CONSCIOUS OF WHERE WE ARE

Being more and more sensitive to, conscious of, aware of, these stages in one's progression through life is a matter of what I call GOING CONSCIOUS. The matter of being quite conscious of the stages we are in (and may or may not be moving through), is key in sensing where we are, *in becoming increasingly aware of the emotional terrain we are traveling.*

When working on emotional and behavioral change (such as change in addicted thinking and behavior), this heightened awareness brings increasing power to our involvement in the processes going on *not only in our own lives, but right there in our own brains*. As so much of what our brains and their programmings are doing for and to us are deep down, under the radar, out of our conscious awareness, the more we can consciously engage with (and monitor) our brains and minds, the more say we can have in our thoughts, feelings, and behaviors. As I have detailed in earlier chapters of this book (*Chapters* 2 and 4, for example), problem addiction is an opportunistic invasive program that moves in on us, on the level of our brain functions, right into our identity and will. Eventually this addiction programming has even us believing we are this programming, this addiction itself.

THESE STAGES ARE PATTERNS

The four basic stages I define in the previous chapter (struggle, paradox, insight, elevation) are patterns, actually are *stages of pattern expression.* We move into and through these stages again and again. We can allow ourselves to recognize the nature of the stages we are in, to see the patterns being expressed in each of these stages. We can learn to see what is involved in moving the energy of a stage we are in to a new level or new use of that energy, and a new stage, or to the same stage in a new way.

We can ever more consciously see the patterns we live (including the patterns of problem addictions), the patterns that dominate and or at least affect our lives. To do so, being sensitive to the stages we move through helps bring us more and more into our own awareness. Developing this sensitivity to ourselves, and to our progression/s or non-progressions through stages, allows us ever more conscious involvement in and say over our personal processes.

We gain more conscious awareness of what our invader, our problem addiction programming, is doing under the radar, out of our conscious awareness. This takes place by being conscious of what we are generally not paying much if any attention to. This allows us to pull information about ourselves up from the subconscious level where addiction programming operates on us, and operates us.

MAPPING HELPS US SENSE AND SEE MORE

Here is where mapping the stages we have been and are moving through in our lives can be quite useful. This pulls our brain's attention and sensitivity to the patterns we are living in and through. This also allows us ever more conscious say in what stage or stages we choose to strive for, what stage or stages we prefer to move out of, what stage or stages we can learn from, *what stage or stages we can harvest energy from*, and more.

MAPPING EXERCISE

I invite clients to begin by drawing very general overview maps of the past year of their lives -- to begin to use the four basic stages as a model for mapping their lives. Many clients feel they do best to do a map of just the past month of their lives, or the past week. Some wish to map the past day. I explain that all levels of mapping, of self inquiry, are very useful. All of this pulls our brain's attentional process to awareness of personal patterns. Ultimately, many clients go on to develop maps of a lifetime, a decade, a year, a month, a week, a day. Some are ready to map the shifting of emotional sensations and patterns of the past hour of their lives, ready to be this aware and to look this closely. All these levels of self awareness are welcome. Some clients will even add sub patterns to each of the four stages, such as different degrees of struggle patterns. These are also welcome. Many clients are also ready to map their long term and even recent recovery processes.

MAPPING OUR STAGES:
SEEING OUR PROGRESSIONS

Some clients see their lives as continuous struggle, as in this map on the following page.:

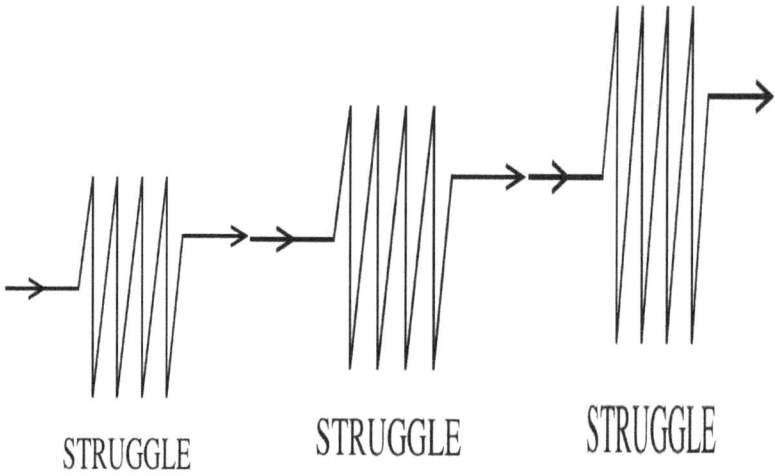

STRUGGLE   STRUGGLE   STRUGGLE

Some clients feel they move back and forth between struggle stages and trapped or stuck paradox stages, as in this map:

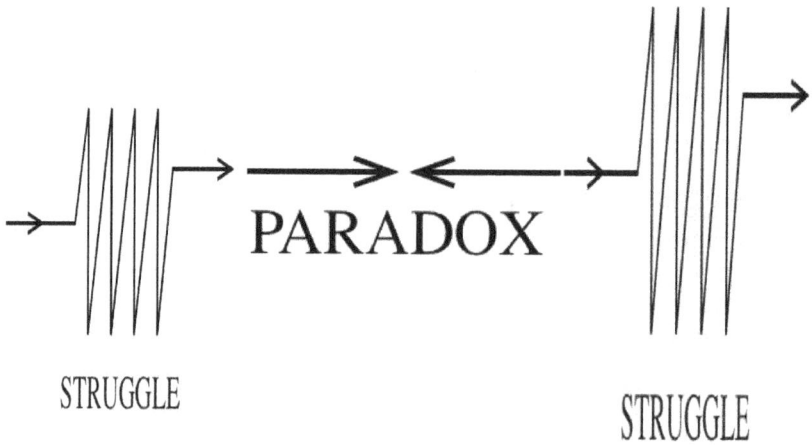

STRUGGLE

PARADOX

STRUGGLE

Other clients say they have felt they were stuck or trapped for a long time, as in this map:

PARADOX

And there are clients who draw very long and or very large maps with repeating periods of the sort of progression below. These clients explain that once in a while they felt some hope or insight, even felt they could use the insight to elevate out of what I call the *pattern trap* of various struggle and paradox stages, but found themselves repeatedly falling back into old patterns of repeating old struggle and paradox stages, as in this map on the following page:

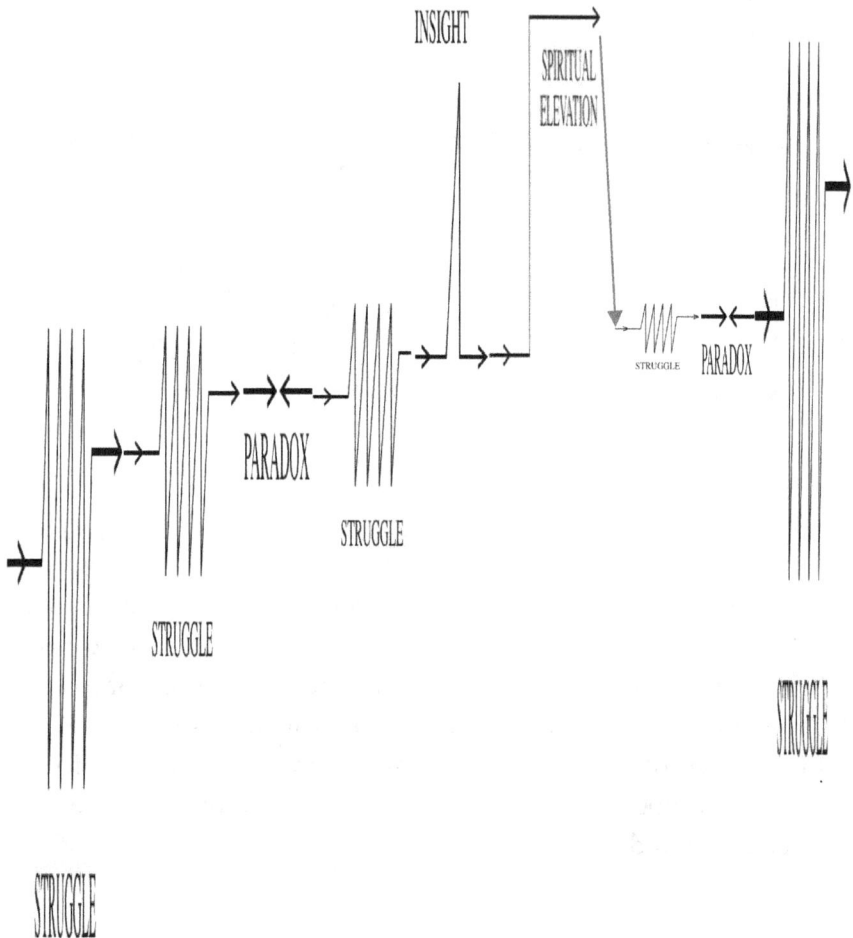

STRUGGLE

STRUGGLE

PARADOX

STRUGGLE

INSIGHT

SPIRITUAL
ELEVATION

STRUGGLE

PARADOX

STRUGGLE

232

Once maps are developed, and the practice of mapping overall and also shorter time periods is started, then this model of understanding is reshared:

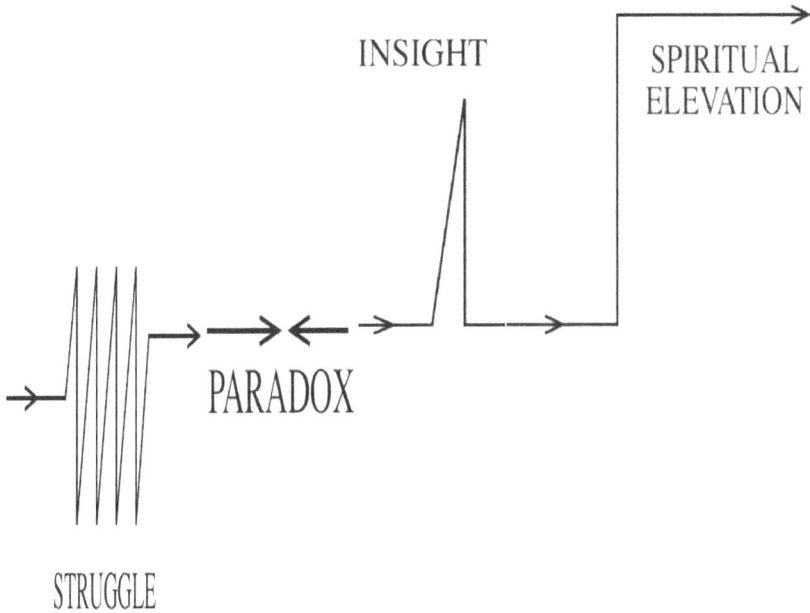

INSIGHT

SPIRITUAL
ELEVATION

PARADOX

STRUGGLE

In this above progression, each stage builds to the next. We can learn to *harvest the energy of each stage* to propel us to the next stage. Hence struggle has value when it can lead to a *productive paradox*, which has value when its energy can *propel an insight*, which has value when that insight may be *sustained or build to an elevation of awareness and understanding.*

Learning to map our journey allows us more conscious say in our journey, engages our mind/brain in otherwise mostly sub- and un- conscious progressions through life and through addictions. The more we can *call our awareness to the subtle aspects of ourselves*, the more say we can have in these otherwise unseen levels of what our brain and (healthy and problem addiction) programmings are doing.

IDEAL STAGE PROGRESSION MAP

Of course, life can be the following progression of ever more aware repeats of this ideal stage progression map (below). As we can learn to consciously move through the four stages, we can learn to master our own emotional, cognitive, and behavioral patterns as they appear in each of these stages.

**Here stage progression becomes ever more conscious.
Here are continuing stage repeats,
yet the stages are moving to
ever higher levels of understanding and awareness
of this process of conscious engagement
in our life patterns:**

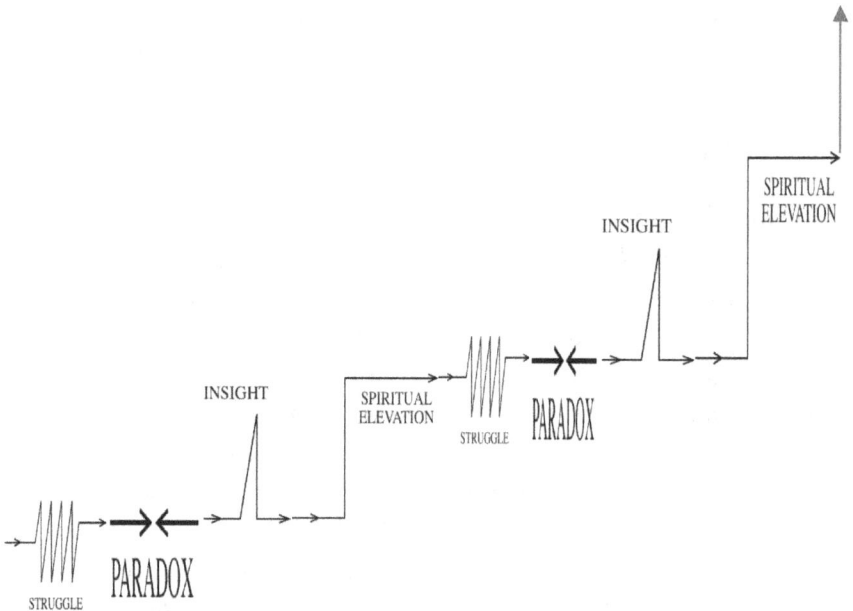

21
Recognizing and Facing
Ingrained Problem Pattern Addiction

I faced my future as I stood and stared.
Then out of the darkness there came
another image of myself to see
with features exactly the same as me.
All at once it became so clear
my life was really on the line.
I knew that if I really wanted to live
I'd have to see my life as mine.

Anonymous Group Therapy Participant

Throughout this book, I have described problem addiction as an invasive opportunistic programming, driving parts of our generally functional healthy programming, even the function of our brains, to run far afield, extremely awry.

IMPORTANT NOTE: I strongly recommend and advise that practitioners, psychotherapists, clinicians, counselors, guides, who utilize these *Gestalting Addiction Processes,* and any other intensive therapy processes, in their work with clients and patients advise clients and patients up front and at all points during these processes, that this deep work is not a one time never need look again experience, that there can be long term realizations that surface far later, that this is the beginning of a lifetime of addressing far and deeply reaching issues that must be addressed on an ongoing basis.

RESPONSIBILITY TO LEARN

I have noted, as I do for clients, that my definition of addiction (being an invader, an invasive program, not part of who we truly are) does *not* mean that persons experiencing problem addiction have no responsibility for addressing the problem. Their responsibility is to learn as much about themselves, about who they truly are, and to allow their actual selves to stand up to the invasive problem addiction patterning. **(Problem addiction, I see you, I know what you are doing here. I will work to defeat you, and to become more of WHO I AM AND YOU ARE NOT: MY *SELF*.)**

TALK TO THE ADDICTION

Whether metaphor or actuality, the mind can work with this concept:

This perception of problem addiction speaks to the individual client *as well as to the invasive problem addiction itself*. And, I have felt so very strongly so very many times, that I am speaking yes, to a client experiencing a problem addiction, and then also to that problem addiction itself.

MODELING THE PROCESS

From time to time, I ask a psychotherapy client (a client who says he or she would like to work with this "metaphor") to visualize moving the problem addiction pattern outside of him or her SELF, over to a chair some distance away from where the client is sitting. I offer to model what might be done, and some clients like this. I motion that I am pulling something out of myself (often from right in front of my heart area, sometimes out of my forehead area) and then actually taking it over to an empty chair somewhere in the room.

SEPARATING FROM THE ADDICTION

Then I return to my chair. Actually, quite often, I go ahead and place my chair over near the problem addiction's chair, so that my chair is facing the problem addiction in its own chair. Then I sit in my chair, facing the problem addiction. I allow my demonstration of this to be humorous if this is received best to begin the process. I begin a conversation, speaking to my problem addiction, "I have moved you out of myself to talk to you. Stay where I put you."

AGREEING TO SAFETY TOOLS

Many clients choose to go ahead and give this a try. Before they begin, we agree that I or they can stop the process at any point, just by saying, "I am stopping this now." Or I or we can call a "time out" to pause or entirely stop the process. Once the stopping and time out agreements are made, we begin. Many clients agree that to begin with, they want to treat this, "like a play, and pretend this is acting, not really happening." This proves to be a safe way to begin for many.

GIVING THE ADDICTION CHARACTERISTICS

Some clients choose to give this problem addiction pattern (this presence, this problem addiction programming) a face or other "human" or "animal" characteristic/s. Other clients choose to give this pattern some kind of shape or form. Sometimes clients choose to draw or scribble something symbolic of the problem addiction and literally take it over to a chair some distance away, and place it there.

SEEING THE STRUGGLE

Of note is how frequently clients act out, either as what they choose to call "a play" or "play acting," or as what they say is something they feel is "really happening right now," a **separation struggle.** They report that the problem addiction is fighting with them when they try to pull it out of themselves. Others say that the problem addiction pattern "keeps trying to get back into me." Some clients choose to act out this struggle between themselves and their addictions. This struggle sometimes continues for several minutes (or longer). Clients know that they can stop or pause the process as they have earlier agreed to the stop and time out tools.

GUIDING THE PROCESS

The psychotherapist guiding this process must remain highly alert at all moments of this process, calling a "time out" or an "I am stopping this now" or a "freeze" whenever safety appears to be an issue. Sometimes pausing the process and checking in is what is needed. Many clients will want to try this again, and this is acceptable. Ask clients to agree not to conduct this on their own at this point in learning, and not to guide others in doing this.

SPEAKING TO THE PROBLEM ADDICTION

Once this imagination and even visualization is working for the client, the client and I speak to this problem addiction pattern. Often, the client describes this problem addiction pattern, sometimes even describing its characteristics as a life form or intelligence of its own -- almost as a sentient being, a stubborn one, resisting not only having to stand (sit) outside the client's body, but also **being resistant regarding being identified in the first place.**

Dialog begins between the client and this addiction.

At this point in the process, many clients speak to their addictions. "I hate you," "leave me alone," "get away from me," "look what you're doing to me," and other statements are made, sometimes shouted or cried. This is the beginning of the clients talking to their addictions. This is also the start of the clients conceptually differentiating themselves from their addictions.

Note: A continuation of this process is described in Chapter 24.

BOUNDARIES MATTER

Many times, clients engaging in this exercise comment that they are having difficulties warding off the addiction pattern's return to their bodies and brains. Here is where a discussion and practice of *defending one's boundaries* is essential.

SEEING AND DEFINING BOUNDARIES

*I frequently have clients do what I call the **personal boundary exercise**. This involves standing or sitting up with room to stretch their arms out in all directions. Clients are asked to draw invisible but very real boundaries around themselves, with those boundaries defined by their hands being out at arm's length from their bodies. Years after this exercise, I hear from clients they are still reminding themselves of their personal boundaries by reaching out and defining their personal space as that within arm's length of their bodies.*

SEEING AND DEFINING INNER BOUNDARIES

*For those who are ready, we take this exercise out of the physical into the mind, and draw boundaries even around metaphorical cells, or for some around their **selves** or **souls**.*

When working on the processes described on the previous and following pages, the concept of clients moving their problem addictions out of themselves to confront them, having personal boundaries defined, strong, and clear, is quite valuable, even essential. These boundaries between themselves and their problem addictions can be ever more distinct and strong with time.

CONTINUE THIS WORK

The exercise (described earlier in this chapter) can be done intensely in a two or three day workshop, or can become a long term process, with some clients coming back to do more work like this regularly, beginning a week or a month or even years later. I always advise clients that they do best to continue to work, even over the years, on the matters raised during these *Gestalting Addiction Processes.*

WE ARE NOT OUR ADDICTIONS

I emphasize to clients experiencing problem addictions that *we are not our problem addictions, even when our identities appear to have been subsumed in varying degrees by these addictions.* I invite clients to step up to the challenge, for many the challenge of their lives, to **unravel themselves** from the problem addiction programming whose goal is to overtake them, their will, their attention selection, decision making, moral judgement, and other (brain) functions.

While problem addiction is not a science fiction-like invasion of us by an off planet life form (as in the film, *Invasion of the Pod People*[74])

---

[74] The 2007 science fiction film, *Invasion of the Pod People,* was a remake of an earlier 1956 film, *Invasion of the Body Snatchers. Invasion of the Pod People* tells the story of the invasion of a town in California following a meteor shower. The film's lead character then notices that people around her are changing, that they seem not to be themselves any longer. She eventually finds that a race of mind-controlling off planet life forms, Pod People, who grow in large seed pods, have invaded and are invading people's bodies and minds. At one point, the horrified lead character is encouraged by Pod People to become an invaded person, to surrender, to come on over to their side, as everything is fine there. The parallels to the invasive problem addiction programming I describe in this book are clear.

the metaphor is valuable. This allows us to see ourselves as invaded by something alien to ourselves, in this case, the invasive problem addiction pattern.

Furthermore, once the problem addiction sets in, *we may become so well invaded that we believe we are who we have become after being invaded,* one of the Pod People, or one of the problem addiction people. In this sense, problem addiction works somewhat like a retro-virus, in that the invading programming or matrix moves into us, its programming becoming part of us, becoming us. *This can make it quite difficult for us to "expel" a problem addiction, as this gives us the sensation of choosing to expel ourselves from ourselves. This seeming retro virus seeks to invade even our identity to make itself ever more difficult to distinguish and extinguish.*

DIS-IDENTIFYING
FROM THE PROBLEM PATTERN

This is where I bring clients to understand (or to consider the possibility) that unravelling, DIS-IDENTIFYING, from their problem addiction pattern must be done.

Addiction, I am not you.
You reside in me, in my mind and body,
hiding within me
as if you are me.

Yet, I see now that you are not me,
and I am not you.

This is the message we can share with clients dealing with problem addiction patterns. They can *conceptually separate themselves* from their problem patterns to isolate these patterns from themselves. They can do so more and more every day.

241

TAKE
OURSELVES BACK

I see the insidious problem addiction patterning as an invasive *and self preserving programming*. As I have noted in earlier chapters, there are times in my psychotherapy office, when I sense, almost see, *the problem pattern in the room,* while I am working with the person this pattern has invaded. This has been a profound and highly informative view of problem patterning afflicting so many of us.

I have at times silently dialoged with the problem addiction pattern program lurking there. I have actually done so many times, witnessed this ADDICTION MATRIX. When I did, I felt I was coming face to face with a powerful, fierce, and strange, almost foreign, intelligence, one that actively sought to block my discovery, detection, recognition, of its presence. I have sensed the power and hegemony of that pattern and its programming. I feel what my clients are dealing with. I may tell a client I am so doing, or wait to do so. Some clients want to hear what I am saying, and if so I share this (although I may filter it somewhat). I get to know this monster, this problem addiction programming, seeking to invade humanity where ever it can.

In working with clients who arrive in my office, some after more than a decade of active problem addiction pattern expression, I see how deeply invasive this programming can be. I see that once this problem addiction patterning is so deeply instilled, entrenched, *this programming is itself programmed to reprogram whatever of our brain functions it can partially or completely usurp.* (I have witnessed several of my clients finding that it took them at least two years of sobriety, after ten or more years of drinking and drugging, to feel that their brains were "just now starting to work again," both cognitively and emotionally.)

GOING CONSCIOUS
IS BECOMING
MORE AND MORE AWARE

Many persons experiencing problem addictions have felt this, have felt the problem addiction pattern seeking to preserve itself, and even seeking to expand itself, even to the detriment of its host – of US. *We must seek to differentiate ourselves from problem addiction programming* when this programming can harm us, confuse us, disguise as us.

The more aware, THE MORE CONSCIOUS, we can be of what is taking place within us, the more we can have a say in what we think, feel, and do. Hence, *going conscious of the presence and effects of invasive problem addiction patterning* is key in addressing problem addiction.

22
Undrugging
The Feelings

Going conscious is like turning on a light. Of course, some lights are on dimmer switches, which means the light will grow as we learn to increase it (or may dim if we don't). We go conscious and see more, and more and more as we continue to go ever more conscious.

The power and potency of our continuously going ever more conscious is great, so great that there may be forces and factors that are driven to suppress this emerging *aware consciousness*[75] we can generate within ourselves.

As discussed earlier in this book, *a self preserving problem addiction program seeks to suppress the power of its host—of us. In so doing, the problem addiction program seeks to suppress our ability to be conscious of its presence, of its actual agenda.* (See *Chapters 9,13*, and *21*, for example.)

---

[75] Again see the book, *UNVEILING THE HIDDEN INSTINCT*, where I define the *aware consciousness*, and include exercises for generating this. See also the book, *THE GOING CONSCIOUS PROCESS*. These books are listed in the booklist at the end of this present book, *GESTALTING ADDICTION*.

IMPORTANT NOTE: I strongly recommend and advise that practitioners, psychotherapists, clinicians, counselors, guides, and others who utilize my *Gestalting Addiction Processes*, and any other intensive therapy processes, in their work with clients and patients advise clients and patients (and any others) up front and at all points during these processes, that this deep work is not a one time never need look again experience, that there can be long term realizations that surface far later, that this is the beginning of a lifetime of addressing far and deeply reaching issues that must be addressed on an ongoing basis.

UNPACKING THE OVERWHELM

Group therapy clients share their experiences and their feelings before and with each other, and discover that they are not alone. They can also learn to listen very closely to themselves and to each other, even to dissect their and others' emotions and problems into manageable parts. I call this *unpacking a problem to see it*.

Clients can learn that their own and others' situations, experiences, sensations, perceptions, even emotions, can be unpacked, viewed in segments, considered step by step, bit by bit. This can be learned in group and or individual therapy or workshop experiences.

Psychotherapists, clinicians, and other guides, can learn what it means to UNPACK THE OVERWHELM, and how to successfully and safely guide this process. When UNDRUGGING FEELINGS, the overwhelm itself can be overwhelming. In working with clients who are undrugging themselves and unpacking emotions, I always make sure to teach my *stop the clock, time out,* and *freeze* functions to everyone so there is always a way to pause or lower the angst when needed. I note that I too may use these tools while working with them. This adds to the perceived safety of the process.

In group therapy and workshop settings, a shared discovery can take place, a view of the **possibility of manageability** of what at times can appear overwhelmingly impossible to control (such as sensations and emotions playing out in problem addiction and recovery processes).

For the individual, this experience of manageability of emotion and then behavior is a cognitive and an emotional movement toward **increased conscious control** of one's mental and emotional processes, **increased cognitive power, even metacognitive power**.

ANOTHER SIDE

There is another side to this story: What we may be overwhelmed by may not be what is actually taking place. Let's back up a minute. …. The brain is constantly completing pictures for us, taking what pieces of the whole of reality it has and completing (estimating, composing, fabricating) the "whole" picture for us. This means that any sense we have of what is going on, including any overwhelm we may be feeling in response to what we believe is going on around us or within us, is the product of the brain's gestalt from pieces of our reality to a sense of the whole reality.

So what is it that is overwhelming when this is happening to a brain inhabited by a problem addiction program? Could it be the infected gestalt, the infected completion to generate the problem addiction determined picture? Yes. (See *Chapters 2* and *8*, for example.) Recall this diagram offered earlier in this book (pictured on the following page):

FORM,
perception,
cognition,
emotion,
response,
REALITY
COMPLETION

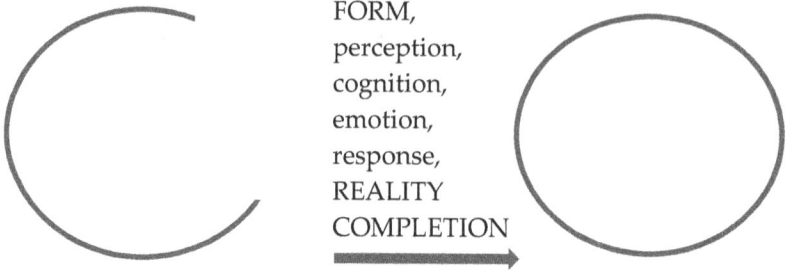

Could the infected gestalt seek to fuel the sense of overwhelm so as to hold the individual in, or spill the individual right back into, the problem addiction cycle (Circle **B** on the following page)? Yes.

**INFECT THE FORM COMPLETION GESTALT
TO OVERWHELM US, SO AS TO CONTROL US:
TO SPILL US BACK INTO THE CYCLE WE ARE CAUGHT IN**

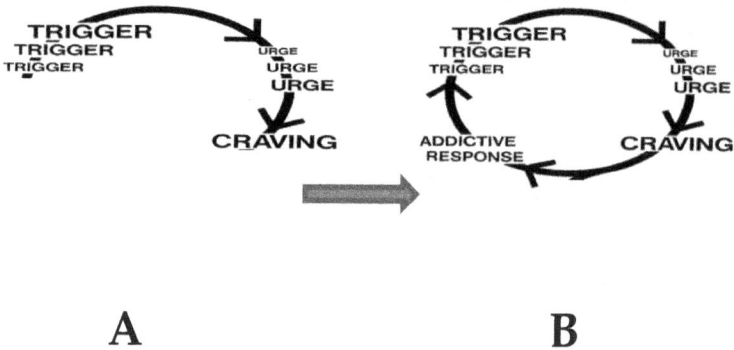

TRIGGER
TRIGGER
TRIGGER

URGE
URGE
URGE

CRAVING

TRIGGER
TRIGGER
TRIGGER

URGE
URGE
URGE

ADDICTIVE
RESPONSE

CRAVING

A   **B**

trigger-to-craving picture of "partial" cycle, of not using the drug (A)
is completed by addictive response going to "whole" cycle, of using the drug
(B)

THIS (B) IS AN INFECTED GESTALT AT WORK
(infected by the problem addiction pattern program)
Circle B =addictive response = relapse or drift toward relapse

ENCOUNTERING
THE EMOTIONS

Many persons experiencing problem addictions have made a habit of drugging, burying, blurring, and or distracting themselves from their feelings. There is a substituting of the addiction roller coaster ride for sober reality – for the real ups and downs of real life.

So many have described their experience of moving into sobriety as both wonderful and daunting, at times even overwhelming. They frequently report that for the first time in years, and for some the first time in decades, they are "coping with life without the blanket or buffer of drugs and alcohol." Now actual emotions are being experienced. At times, these emotions can be wonderful. However, many clients describe their *undrugged* experiences facing insecurity, sadness, fear, anger, confusion, frustration, and other emotions as, "So intense I almost wanted to drug myself again," and or, "Too much for me so I went back to drinking and drugging just to cope."

Note that when age at first use of the drug/s (yes, again alcohol is a drug) was in childhood or adolescence, the brain may not have been able to (allowed to) undergo *key developmental phases undrugged*. Hence, the undrugged, unimpeded, *management of emotions* may not have been experienced and fully developed. Some of my clients tell me they are certain that they are examples of "emotionally arrested development." They express their sense that encountering life unaided by drugs, alcohol, and or the distractions of other addictions such as gambling and gaming, is overwhelming, looks and feels impossible. (Some of these clients began using alcohol/drugs at the age of ten or eleven, or earlier, and then spent their preteen and teenage years, plus their young adult years, and beyond, "under the influence.")

For many of the participants in my *GESTALTING ADDICTION* individual and group therapy sessions, just talking about feelings is a new, or a newly revived, experience. As a person emerges from the haze of drug/alcohol and or other addiction, he or she is barraged by a stream of long overlooked (even raw) sensation and emotion. All too often, the simplest of expressions about the simplest of these feelings is a challenge.

Feeling real feelings, whether positive or negative or neutral, and then talking about these feelings is a skill that may have to be learned or relearned. A group process is a good environment for this learning and relearning as there is validation and support in the shared experience. There is also a safe environment to discover and share emotions that may be surfacing for the first time or the first time in years.

Working with clients as they are undrugging themselves requires careful attention, as these clients are experiencing at times new, at times old and stuffed away, emotions with increasing veracity and intensity. This requires attention to clients' responses to hitherto "unfelt" (as one client described this), or previously not fully recognized, or not yet managed, emotions. Even *rehearsing the management of emotions* in therapy settings, and doing so many times along the way, is very useful (for example, anger management practice).

UNBUNDLING EMOTIONS

I frequently keep a chart of faces, hundreds of faces expressing hundreds of emotions, handy. I have been told by clients, "I thought all these emotions were just anger. Now I realize there are many feelings I've been having. Some are anger, some are sadness, some are loneliness, some are frustration, some are shame and other feelings. Yes, there is some happiness in there too, but it gets mixed in with the bad feelings. Like a giant soup."

The tendency to collapse all of one's emotions into one or two general bundles is natural. First, this is a ready response to waves of feelings. Second, emotions that have never been addressed or even defined may have no other label in the mind than a simple grouping into "good or bad feeling," or "happy or sad feeling," or "not mad versus mad feeling." While we tend to see and even expect this bundling of emotions in very young children, less appreciation for the adult version of this bundling is available (yet is essential).

Back to unpacking the overwhelm -- clients can learn to safely unpack and manage the bundles of emotion they may be carrying. A safe environment in which to express emotion is first and foremost necessary. Group and or individual therapy settings can offer this safety. As issues are touched upon that bring forth the expression of emotion, allow this emotion, encourage it, let it cry or shout or otherwise talk itself out.

Once there is a pause in this expression, the psychotherapist can begin a gentle directing of re-examining what has been felt in terms of its bits. Emotions have pieces too. The raw expression of raw overwhelm has been invited. Now the expression of pieces of this overall feeling can be invited.

REMINDER
REGARDING POWER TOOLS

Gestalt and other psychotherapy processes conducted with clients as they are undrugging their emotions, undrugging themselves, can take place short term, prior to recovery, or a short time into recovery, or as an ongoing even lifelong process. Ideally this process is ongoing. These clients are *downloading*, releasing, expressing, discovering, emotions that are now surfacing, and will continue to surface. More and more, these emotions are being experienced unaided by alcohol and drugs and other problem addition objects/behaviors.

The psychotherapist or other clinician must be highly aware of the *undrugging emotions experiences problem addicted clients face*. As noted in the early chapters of this book, when engaging in intense and incisive, deep reaching, psychotherapy such as gestalt therapy, the psychotherapist/clinician/guide does best to move carefully, in steps, checking in with the client at every point along the way to see how deeply and intensively the client wishes to, and actually is ready to, work.

23
The Going Conscious Process

This *Gestalting Addiction Process* I offer my clients is quite subtle yet distinctly profound. As discussed in depth in the first five parts of this book, I have developed this approach according to my view that *problem addiction is an opportunistic and invasive pattern and program*.

We must address, even speak to, this program, this dangerous matrix, that is invading our minds/brains, that seeks to control us by taking control of our key brain functions such as decision making, moral judgement, attention, impulse control, and more.

> IMPORTANT NOTE: I strongly recommend and advise that practitioners, psychotherapists, clinicians, counselors, guides, and others who utilize these *Gestalting Addiction Processes*, and any other intensive therapy processes, in their work with clients and patients (and others) advise clients and patients (and others) up front and at all points during these processes, that this deep work is not a one time never need look again experience, that there can be long term realizations that surface far later, that this is the beginning of a lifetime of addressing far and deeply reaching issues that must be addressed on an ongoing basis.

In that problem addiction programming has invaded the SELF, woven its tendrils into the operation of the brain and body, *even into the identity*, we are also having to gestalt *ourselves* — or at least the areas of ourselves infected by problem addiction (areas that are difficult to separate from the whole of ourselves).

DIFFICULT TO DISTINGUISH

We may be at the point where we cannot entirely distinguish between ourselves and the problem addiction programming that has invaded us (as individuals and as a species). This *vague boundary between ourselves and our problem addiction programming* fuels the problem addiction while it is infecting and seeking ever more control over us.

I strongly suggest that our defense, our strategy to take ourselves back, to strengthen ourselves from further incursion into who we are, is to keenly heighten our awareness, to become EVER MORE CONSCIOUS of what is happening to us, what is taking place in our minds and brains.

RETRIEVAL OF THE SELF

So, this *Going Conscious Process* I have developed works on so many levels of ourselves. This is a conceptual and cognitive, as well as emotional and spiritual, process. This *going conscious* is a rediscovery of the self.[76] In fact, this is in essence a process of…

retrieving the self from what has occluded the self, such as a problem addiction pattern program.

---

[76] I offer further discussion of and exercises regarding this matter in these books: *KEYS TO PERSONAL DISCOVERY* and also *THE GOING CONSCIOUS PROCESS*, as well as in *UNVEILING THE HIDDEN INSTINCT*, all listed in the recommended reading at the end of this present book, *GESTALTING ADDICTION*.

The more clarity we have regarding ourselves, who we actually are, the more sensitive to and committed to our actual selves we are, the greater the strength we have to retrieve our SELVES from problem addiction programming—to pull ours SELVES out of that invasive problem addiction matrix.

Refining our contact with ourselves is like turning on an internal microscopic scanner. However, we are not looking at biological elements, per se, we are more looking at our sense of our**selves**, our sense of who we actually are,[77] the micro-mini moments of our ongoing existence. For it is there, under our own radar, below the level of our *aware consciousness*, that problem addiction inhabits us.

BEING CONSCIOUS, YET MORE CONSCIOUS

To allow clients to move closer in to themselves, for example, to have more awareness of what is taking place in their minds and bodies when they are feeling their problem addiction patterning activating/reactivating, I have introduced this *Going Conscious Process* throughout these chapters of *Part Six* of this book. Indeed, each of the chapters of *Part Six* is an element of both the *Going Conscious Process* and the *Gestalting Addiction Process*, as these work together.

Of course, we are all conscious if we are even asking ourselves whether or not we are conscious. However, consciousness is a many splendored state. Being conscious of the difference between night and day or hot and cold may not guarantee being conscious of the early indications that one's problem addiction pattern is right

---

[77] As noted herein, I further develop this sense of who we are in *UNVEILING THE HIDDEN INSTINCT*. See the recommended reading listed at the end of this present book, *GESTALTING ADDICTION*.

there, calling for its activation/reactivation – in obvious trigger-craving ways, yet also in very subtle brain function invasion ways.

It is heightened and trained awareness of oneself
that can bring greater control
over automatic behaviors and functions.

This heightened awareness can generate
increased conscious control
over brain functions such as decision making, attention,
moral judgement, impulse control, and more.

MAKING
EXECUTIVE CONTROL
AND METACOGNITION
UNDERSTANDABLE
AND ACCESSIBLE
TO EVERYONE

The brain's
thought process management system,
the executive control function (ECF),
can be re-owned.
We can reach in and
take greater control
of our ECF.

Our ECF generally runs automatically on our un- and sub-conscious levels. However, I have found that our ECF can be consciously put to work to take ourselves, our brain functions, back from the invasive problem addiction programming. Consciously being more aware of, and then working with, our brain's ECF opens pathways into ourselves that allow for change.

This is going to be a metacognitive process, a conscious metacognitive process. (See *Chapter 5* as well as the footnote below.).[78] Clients can learn what this process means and how to further and consciously activate their metacognitions. *(I delve into this in workshops and therapy sessions, more deeply than on these pages. Note that metacognition is "thinking about thinking," being "aware of one's awareness," having an awareness and understanding of one's own thought processes.)*

AWARENESS

Awareness, while generally present in daily life, is far more than what we tend to think of as awareness. Awareness is a key element in heightened and empowered consciousness. Again, I note that heightened awareness is our greatest defense against an invasive patterning, an opportunistic program such as problem addiction.

As these terms, *awareness* and *consciousness*, tend to overlap in general usage, let me distinguish between these for purposes of

---

[78] One of my earlier books, *LEARNING TO LEARN*, and my earlier works on **metacognition** conducted in that same time period, are in essence all about *thinking about thinking* and *being aware of one's awareness*, of one's thought processes. For more on *being aware of awareness*, see *UNVEILING THE HIDDEN INSTINCT*, and *THE GOING CONSCIOUS PROCESS*, as well as *KEYS TO PERSONAL DISCOVERY*. See reading list at the end of this present book, *GESTALTING ADDICTION*.

this discussion. We do have a consciousness. This consciousness apparently extends through all of what is called our un-conscious(ness) and our sub-conscious(ness), right up to our *conscious conscious(ness)*. In the latter category, I suggest there are several sub-levels of this level, this *conscious* consciousness.

What I am here calling **conscious consciousness**, is our daily consciousness: I am somewhat awake, I am relatively alert, I am paying some attention, etc. Certainly we can be and are generally aware we are conscious.

However, having what I describe as an *aware consciousness*[79] at work is another level, an ever more heightened level, of consciousness. This this a level I seek to inspire clients to aim for. It is here, in the realm of the *aware* consciousness, that we can "see" (feel, sense, know) ever more of what is going on around and within us, including within our minds/brains.

MOST IMPORTANTLY
BEGIN BY
BECOMING
AWARE OF AWARENESS ITSELF

Becoming more and more aware of one's awareness is best done in increments. First, it is important to become highly aware of awareness itself, as I demonstrate to my clients by guiding them through this process:

---

[79] See further discussion of the *aware consciousness* in KEYS TO PERSONAL DISCOVERY and in UNVEILING THE HIDDEN INSTINCT; both these books are listed in recommended reading at the end of this present book, GESTALTING ADDICTION.

1) To become directly *aware of your consciousness*, begin with your awareness: grow ever more *aware of your awareness* **itself.**

2) Take a moment to focus on your awareness. This is *not* about focusing on what you are "aware *of*," such as the person across the room, or the car racing down the street outside your window, or the cake baking in the oven. This is about being *aware of awareness itself*.

3) Sit with your awareness a while. ***Do not be meditating, do not be hypnotized, do not drug yourself.*** This requires a high level of alertness. The more awake and aware you are right now, the better. Notice yourself being aware.

4) Now fine tune your awareness, saying: "Hello awareness, I see you here, being aware of things taking place. Yet now I also see you here, *just being awareness itself*."

5) Feel yourself ***aware of being aware*** of nonphysical and non-emotional essences. No need to define these, simply draw your awareness to what else there is to be aware of beyond the first sensations that race in, such as air temperature, hunger, physical desire, etc.

6) This is a ***self scan*** for levels of knowing and being beyond the explicit obvious emotional and physical realms. Become increasingly aware of subtle sensations, even seeming flows of energy, and patterns of energy, whatever these seem to be to you. Make notes on this. Do this scan once in a while, making notes on increasing awareness.

7) Track your increasing awareness of sensations you have not been previously aware of, especially those non-physical and non-emotional sensations and awarenesses.

Note: I define awareness as the ***aware and operant*** element of the consciousness. As simple as is the notion of awareness, this is a powerful resource we have yet to far more fully develop. Our heightened awareness itself will be key in our survival.[80] Again, this awareness is highly alert, not asleep, or meditating, or hypnotized, or drugged in some way.

GOING CONSCIOUS
BEYOND MINDFULNESS

A popular teaching quite common in addiction treatment and other fields is the notion of "mindfulness." Mindfulness has been quite a useful teaching for many, and there is no discounting of this here. Mindfulness teachings include meditation and other similar exercises designed to reduce stress, assist with "healing" processes, and activate compassion, for example.

The *Going Conscious Process* I offer in this (and other of my books[81]) differs significantly from general mindfulness teachings. The *Going Conscious Process* calls for a purposefully highly alert, even metacognitive, and distinctly non-meditative state of mind, calling for a keenly adept and aware state of mind that can sense, detect, confront, even reverse, AND GESTALT invasive problem addiction programming.

---

[80] I explain this further in *UNVEILING THE HIDDEN INSTINCT*.

[81] I detail more of my **go conscious** work in my books, *THE GOING CONSCIOUS PROCESS* and *UNVEILING THE HIDDEN INSTINCT*, and *OVERRIDING THE EXTINCTION SCENARIO*, and *KEYS TO PERSONAL DISCOVERY*, among other publications under my last name Brownemiller and also Browne-Miller.

24
Gestalting the Addiction

IMPORTANT NOTE:
I strongly recommend and advise that practitioners, psychotherapists, clinicians, counselors, guides, and others who utilize these *Gestalting Addiction Processes*, and any other intensive therapy processes, in their work with clients and patients (and others) advise clients and patients (and others) up front and at all points during these processes, that this deep work is not a one time never need look again experience, that there can be long term realizations that surface far later, that this is the beginning of a lifetime of addressing far and deeply reaching issues that must be addressed on an ongoing basis.

Let's return to the description of guiding a client in *gestalting addiction* (see first half this description in *Chapter 21*). Here the client is participating in an imagined (or actual, depending on how the client chooses to describe this) differentiation between her or him SELF and the problem addiction pattern.

DIFFERENTIATING

At this point in the process, (first phase described in *Chapter 21*) the client has already moved (conceptually, metaphorically, even emotionally) the notion or image or presence of the problem addiction program out of her or his physical body (out of the SELF) and has put this problem addiction in an empty chair.

Note: Some clients report they cannot "get it to move all the way out of me, it is right here, still hanging on right here." Clients can work with this process in what ever way they feel they can, even if this may require adaptations such as the addiction program being put in the client's hand rather than in a chair several feet away. The psychotherapist continues to monitor to prevent any potential self harm in these processes. Never is a client to use a boffer or even his or her own hand to hit or strike or even threaten his or her own self (or anyone else in the room). No self harm is part of this process.

Returning to and resuming the earlier *addiction in the chair* process:

The client is now seated facing this problem addiction. The "dialog" has started, as this section of the process (shared earlier, in *Chapter 21)* indicates:

*[Now} many clients speak to their addictions: "I hate you," "leave me alone," "get away from me," "look what you're doing to me," and other statements are made, sometimes shouted or cried. This is the beginning of clients **talking to their addictions**. This is also the start of their **conceptually differentiating from their addictions.***

This ***differentiating of themselves from their addictions*** can be in itself intensely emotional. Clients talk about this process, saying, "I know this addiction isn't who I am supposed to be, but it's like now, I've gone on like this so long, it's like all I am is an addict," and, "I am almost afraid to tell my addiction it is not me," and asking,

"If I let my addiction go, what will be left of me?
It has taken so much of me, of who I am,
can I separate myself from it?"

?

SEPARATING

Once moving further into this **notion of separation from the invasive addiction programming,** clients then add to their initial comments, "Wow, this is telling me this might be possible, that someday I will be able take control of my addiction," and "I want to keep practicing this, it helps me see this whole addiction thing differently," and "This gives me some power, a little power for now, and I hope more power over my addiction as this process moves on." As noted in the *Chapter 21* description of this process:

> *Many clients who choose just to observe others taking part in this process find themselves in tears watching. Some of these observers then want to also gestalt their own addictions. Those who proceed with this process move into further communicating with their addictions.*

SPEAKING

Confidence builds. Clients are now feeling that they want to try gestalting, or at least speaking, to their addictions:

> *Clients' communications [with their various addictions] include statements such as, "Addiction, I feel you tugging on me," and, "You are trying to be me," and, "You are getting inside my head. trying to make me follow your orders: trigger, crave, use, trigger crave use, over and over, like you don't want me to escape. It's like I am your slave."*

Engagement in the gestalting process grows:

> *Other clients will choose to move back and forth, sitting first in their own chairs and speaking to their addictions, then sitting in*

their addictions' chairs and speaking back to themselves in their addictions' voices.

DIALOGING

Moving on from the *Chapter 21* description of this opening to the *Gestalting Addiction Process*, the momentum builds. Clients describe and even *voice the dialog* back and forth between themselves and the problem addiction/s they have (imagined that they have, or perhaps actually have, conceptually) moved outside themselves and placed in empty chairs:

> CLIENT: *Addiction, get out of me and stay out.*
>
> ADDICTION: *I will never leave you, I am in control of you.*
>
> CLIENT: *I will fight you for my freedom.*
>
> ADDICTION: *You cannot win. Anytime I want, I can make your cravings so strong you break down.*
>
> CLIENT: *Now that I see you, I know you are not part of me, I can stand up to you.*
>
> ADDICTION: *No you cannot, as I can always take you down. I can even kill you, drive you to kill yourself, overdosing.*
>
> CLIENT: *I will not let you take me down. I see what you are now, you are not part of me, and I can stop you.*

RELEASING

NOTE: *At this point in this particular process being quoted here, this particular client asks whether he might stand up and go over to the addiction and hit it with the padded boffer (padded bat) that had been provided earlier. With permission, the client then does so, and repeatedly hits the "empty chair" where his addiction is "sitting." This continues for several minutes, while the client shouts and cries and hits his addiction.*

COMPLETING
(FOR NOW)

Then the client sits down on the floor in front of the addiction's chair, exhausted, and cries for a while. Everyone in the room remains silent except for their own crying. Several minutes into this, the client stands up, looks at me (the psychotherapist) and says, "The chair is empty now, the addiction seems gone. I don't know where it went, but it is not in the chair or anywhere I can see it, and it is not in me right now. But I will always keep a watch for it, I will always be on the lookout for it trying to take back control."

RECOGNIZING
EMOTIONAL ENGAGEMENT

During the above process, both participating and observing clients are emotionally engaged, sighing, crying, shouting, at times cheering for the client who they see standing up to the addiction pattern program. At times, some clients move into prayer mode.

CONTINUING
TO GUIDE SAFETY

*During this Gestalting Addiction Process, it continues to be the role of the psychotherapist, clinician, and or other guide to monitor for the safety of all participants (and observers) in the room, continuing to offer the earlier referred to (Chapter 21) **stop the process** and **time out** and **freeze options.** Additionally, participants can be asked by the psychotherapist to engage in the **personal boundary exercise*** *(also in Chapter 21) during a **time out** at any point during this process.*

*Also, it is essential to continue to remind all participants that nothing can be thrown at anyone, or moved in a threatening way toward anyone or anything in the room – with the exception of the hitting of an empty chair with the padded bat, and only if this is approved by the therapist in advance of the process. **Note that the therapist, clinician, or guide will never approve threatening to hit or strike or actually hitting or striking oneself or anyone else in the room.** Also, no object can be used unless it is a padded bat (or other safe and approved provided object) aimed only at the specific empty chair. Any object being used will be one the participants have already been trained to use and the psychotherapist, clinician, and or guide has already provided and noted can be used and how this can be used.*

CLOSING
(FOR NOW)

Following a client's "work" or "process" such as the one described above, the psychotherapist, clinician, guide, or other facilitator must conduct:
- *A thorough check in with the particular client who participated in the above process:*
    - *--What are you feeling now – first physically – what are you feeling most about your body. (Some facilitators even check pulse and blood pressure at this time.)*
    - *--What are you feeling now – emotionally. (Have a list of questions ready to address state of mind, mood, concentration, cravings for addictive behaviors, and so on.)*
    - *--What will you be doing the rest of the day or evening, what support systems do you have available, etc. (Have*

a list of support services and systems such as 800 numbers.)

- *A review with the client (and all who are present) of what this process was, what took place, its significance.*
- *A check in with all observers regarding their thoughts on the process and their states of mind and body, and their own support systems.*
- *A group and or individual decompression or other relaxation exercise.*
- *An explanation that this was just a starting introduction to the Gestalting Addiction Process, and that there is much more to this work. Those who feel they want to work more along these lines may inform the psychotherapist, clinician, or other guide that they would like to continue. Clients and patients (and other participants) are reminded that this sort of work must be done with a trained psychotherapist as it reaches quite deeply into the SELF, and are also reminded that deep work like this can bring up issues and emotions after they leave. Hence, be ready to see a therapist or clinician as a follow on to this experience.*

IMPORTANT NOTE:

It is the responsibility of practitioners, psychotherapists, clinicians, guides, and others conducting such processes to inform clients, patients, and other participants that such deep work reaches deeply into the mind and brain, self and soul, and requires expert follow on attention in both the short term and long term.

The above is but one example of a basic *Gestalting Addiction Process*, and does not address in depth additional portions of the above session or other events. This is simply an excerpt serving as an example of *Gestalting Addiction Processes*. The following chapter continues this example of **gestalting addiction**.

25
Addiction Gestalting Itself

Now let's return to the *Gestalting Addiction Process* described in *Chapters 21* and *24*. After observing this process and these specific steps in the *Gestalting Addiction Process* (noted in sections of *Chapter 24*):

> Differentiating
> Separating
> Speaking
> Dialoging
> Releasing
> Completing (for now)
> Closing (for now)…

…there may be a next client ready to do more of the same form of *gestalting addiction* work. The following example describes a similar process, this one where the client moved into a somewhat different level of this work, and had her *addiction gestalt itself*.

NOTE: The psychotherapist, as I do, can model for clients these *Gestalting Addiction Processes*, demonstrate the various levels and intensities of these processes. This modeling can help set the agenda for a next chapter or phase of a therapy process, can open doors to *Gestalting Addiction Processes* that may be logical next steps. However, clients should not be required to participate in any process. In other words, never require or demand (or allow peers or group members to demand) that clients participate.

The problem addiction pattern's program seeks to dominate its host – US—to our detriment. Whether or not this problem addiction pattern program has a conscious "mind" of its own, there is an agenda being implemented by this problem pattern, which is to work its way into, utilize, our brain functions in order to operate and control us.

CLIENTS WHO
WANT TO SPEAK
TO THE PROBLEM ADDICTION

Clients who want to speak to this problem addiction pattern program with its agenda that is so dangerous for us can do (guided by a highly trained psychotherapist, clinician, or other guide) as was described in the previous chapter, first by differentiating then separating from the problem pattern. This is essential as this problem pattern has worked its way so very deeply into persons experiencing problem addiction that it has worked to weave itself into their identities. This attempted (or actual) take over can be reversed, with great awareness.

What does it take to have this problem addiction pattern step out of the shadows, reveal its presence, its invasive program, to us? What does it take to have this insidious problem pattern speak up, actually directly speak to us?

We can work in terms of metaphor to engage in this awareness, to open our minds to this awareness. We have seen, in the previous chapter (*Chapter 24*), an opening processing, which in itself is a conceptual leap for many participants. This is an initial gestalting of this problem addiction pattern.

Now let's take a look at some of the next phases of this gestalting of addiction....

APPRECIATING IMAGINATION AS A TOOL

*I explain to clients that, in order to work with ourselves and the addiction pattern program, we can give the addiction we are speaking to whatever imagined characteristics we choose (such as a face or voice or body or symbol, or all of these). The imagination can offer us creative ways of addressing challenges, challenges such as addressing the **intertwining of the problem addiction program with our otherwise functional brain, ECF, and other neural processes.** It is this intertwining by this invasive problem addiction programming that can harm us, even kill us.*

ALLOWING CLIENTS TO SAY WHEN READY

Some observing clients respond that they have now quietly, internally, started speaking to their own invasive problem addiction patterns. These clients say that they have indeed given these patterns, and these patterns' programmings, voices to help think about dialoging with them. Many say they have already moved at least somewhat into the sort of process described in the previous chapter (Chapter 24).

Some say they are ready to "give this a try." They proceed with the first few steps in the gestalting noted above: differentiating, then separating. ... And then, as some of them begin to move more deeply into this process, something happens....

STRUGGLING TO SEPARATE

*For example, one particular client reports that the differentiation has started out as an **imaginary distinguishing** of the self from the problem addiction, but then something has not worked as she had thought it would: She says there has been an unexpectedly intense **separation struggle**, with the problem addiction pattern* *fighting the separation so intensely the she is tiring simply trying to carry on this separation.*

The client is squirming and clenching her fists. Observers note this and ask if she is alright. She says yes, "But I am fighting this addiction, I have to, I want to, because it won't let me take it out of myself – and I don't want it inside me, running me without my permission, any longer."

At several points during this process, I ask the client if she wants to continue, and or wants to use any particular safety tools (such as the time out, freeze, pause, or deep breathing tools, or the boundary fortifying exercise, etc.). She says, "Thank you, no, I'm OK, I want to do this just this way."

SEPARATING PARTIALLY

Finally, the client chooses to move what she can of the addiction into an empty chair, and to then sit in her chair facing this addiction – while knowing that this addiction is still also inhabiting her as the separation process has not completed.

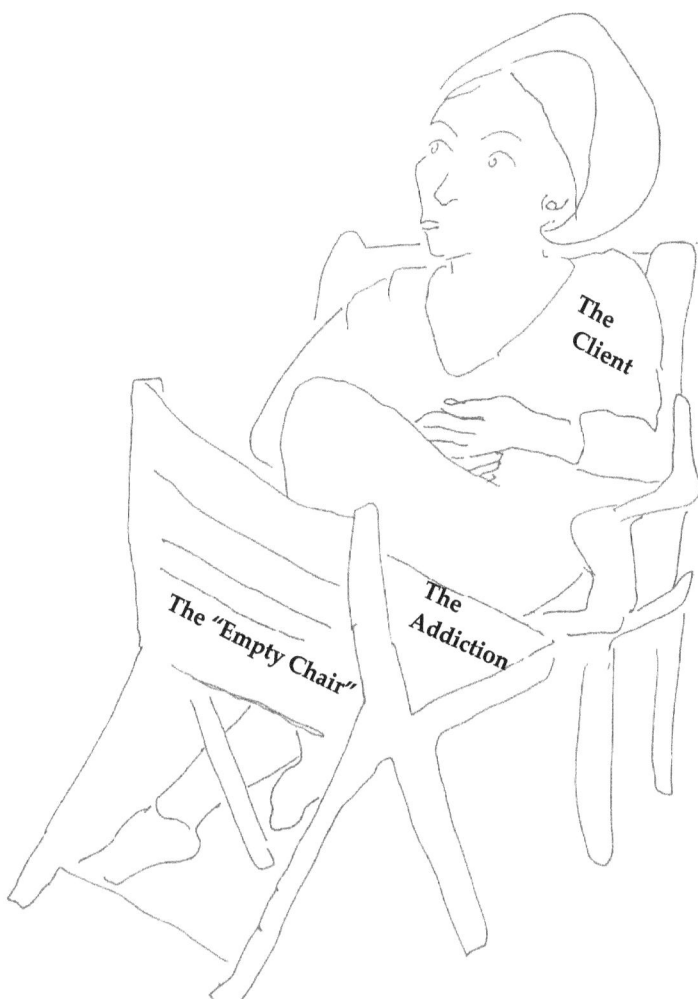

The Client

The Addiction

The "Empty Chair"

ENGAGING IN COMMUNICATION WITH THE ADDICTION

Now it is time for the next steps in this Gestalting Addiction Process: speaking to and dialoging with the addiction pattern program. The client in her chair speaks to the addiction program in its chair: "I can't get you all the way out of me. You have no right to stay in me if I want you out. Why are you still in me?"

The client moves to the addiction's chair and responds, "Because, you fool, I am you. You cannot separate yourself from me."

The client assertively moves back to her own chair to respond, but begins to waver in her certainty that she knows what she wants to say. In this moment, there is a shift in the client's body posture and language. Now the client looks confused and angry as she sits in her own chair and speaks in the addiction's voice: "Hah, I have you now, you fool! I am sitting in both these chairs. You cannot separate from me." The client's demeanor changes. She is suddenly horrified the addiction is speaking from within her. She is crying, yet says to the psychotherapist (to me), "I can do this. I am OK. I want to keep going with this a while. I will stop if it gets too scary for me."

Still upset, the client quickly moves to the addiction's chair, and says, "Well then, I will talk to you from over here. You are in my chair, so I am in yours."

Then the client quickly moves back and forth between the two chairs. She begins to move more and more rapidly, continuing to dialog back and forth.

STOPPING OR PAUSING THE PROCESS

*Then the client stops. She asks me, the psychotherapist, if she can stop, use the **time out tool**, and do some **deep breathing**. I of course say yes. One of the observers suggests she also do the personal boundary exercise, right then. The clients says she will do deep breathing but does not feel safe doing the **boundary exercise** at this time, because she feels the addiction program's "hands" still inside her boundaries, "reaching into me from that chair, or this chair, it keeps changing. Guess this means I need to do boundaries, too, but I can't right now."*

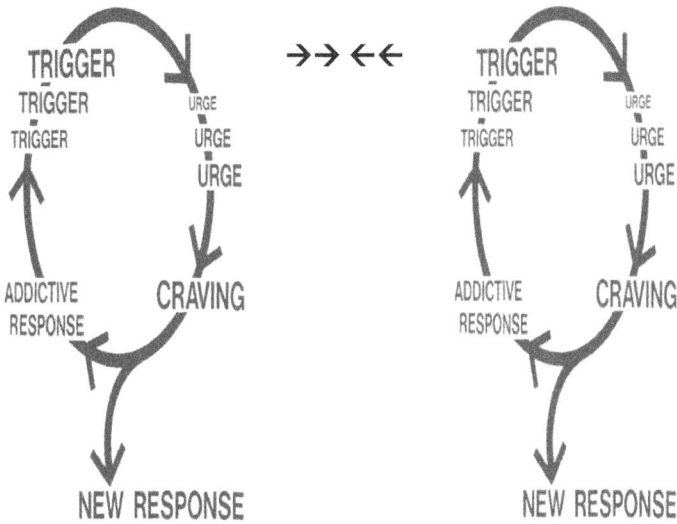

TRIGGER
TRIGGER
TRIGGER
URGE
URGE
URGE
ADDICTIVE RESPONSE
CRAVING

→→ ←←

TRIGGER
TRIGGER
TRIGGER
URGE
URGE
URGE
ADDICTIVE RESPONSE
CRAVING

NEW RESPONSE   NEW RESPONSE

LETTING THE PROBLEM ADDICTION
SIT IN BOTH CHAIRS

*After several minutes of deep breathing, the client says she is ready to continue, that she wants to try to get deeply into the addiction gestalting itself process. She says she wants to hear what this is again. I respond, "**Let the problem addiction sit in both chairs and call itself out, talk to itself, gestalt itself**." She says she is "a little scared" but will, if she feels these are needed, use the **stop the process** and **time out** and **freeze tools** that she learned along with this group (the group who is in the room, observing at this time).*

275

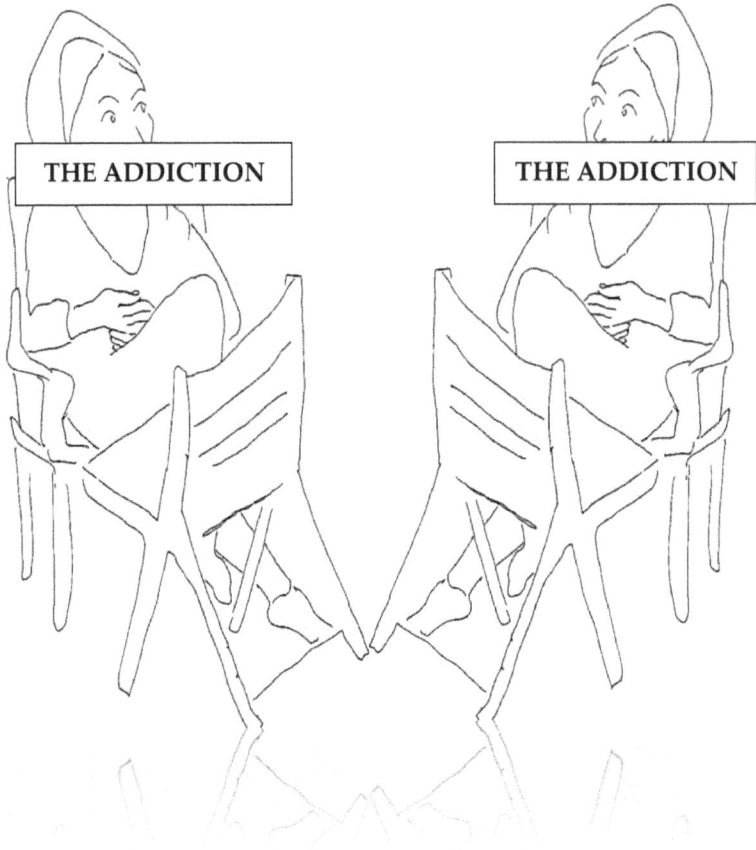

THE ADDICTION   THE ADDICTION

TRYING TO
OUTWIT THE ADDICTION

"I am your addiction," the client says to herself aloud, from her own chair, still sounding confused. Then, she moves over and says back to herself from the addiction's chair, "And I am your addiction, too. Everywhere you look, I will be there, you cannot get away."

The client moans. She does some deep breathing as she moves back to the other chair. But then she stops. She moves the two chairs closer together, still facing each other, but now just a foot apart.

Now she sits in the chair that had been the "other chair." "You are killing this woman." Then she shifts to the other chair, the one that had been her own, quickly answering, "No, we are killing her."

Now the client moves rapidly now, almost leaping back and forth from chair to chair, saying:

> *"No you are."*

> *"No you are."*

> *"Stop this, get out of yourself, get out of me."*

> *"Can't do that, can't get yourself out of yourself, can you?"*

CALLING ON THE GROUP

Puzzled and agitated, the client breaks "out of role" and asks the group, "What do you guys think, what should I do?"

Several group members stand up, come over and hug her. They ask if they can sit on the floor near her. She says yes. She continues with the dialog between the addiction program inhabiting her and what appears to also be this addiction program answering back.

"Those people can't help you, they are addicts, too. You can't help yourself no matter what you do," the client says to herself, now sobbing. She moves to the other chair and cries for a minute.

Then she turns to the group members sitting near her and says, "I'm in trouble. This addiction is both in me and outside of me. **It is talking through me to itself.** I can feel that this is not me talking to it. I am trying to get these two things out of here, but they don't want to leave. I can't get out of this right now."

Now I, the psychotherapist, gesture to my colleague who is sitting among the observers.[82] He nods at me and stands. Then he says to the client who has been moving back and forth between the two chairs, "Wait." Then he turns to me and asks me, "Dr., can I participate in this client's process?" I say with her permission. He then asks the client, "May I come up and participate in your process?" She says yes.

SHIFTING THE
LOCUS OF THE ADDICTION FURTHER OUT

He proceeds. "OK look. Your addiction has taken over both chairs. Will you stay here while I carry these two chairs outside?"

"Yes," she responds. She stands still and silent while this is done. (Later she described this moment as "a time lasting longer than it really did, a time when I felt hollowed out, empty, like someone just robbed me of something. At first I felt like he was taking me out of the room with the chairs, and wanted to follow him, but I did not.")

When my colleague has moved the two chairs outside, he returns and stands silently facing the client. She stands there facing him silently for a few minutes.

---

[82] This colleague has worked with me in several of my *Gestalting Addiction Group Processes*, and has practiced this next step with me several times.

*Then the client almost shouts, "Oh wow. I get it. I wasn't in those chairs you took out of the room. I am **not** those chairs and **not** the addiction that was in those chairs. The addiction had been talking to itself, not to me. I felt at first like you were taking something away from me when you took those two chairs out though. It was like you were taking me away from me. It was weird, I felt robbed, empty. It took a few minutes to bring myself into myself without the addiction there."*

"Yes."

"You moved the two chairs that my addiction was inhabiting out of the room, and I am still in here, standing here alone without them. Thank you. They are not me." Now the client shouts with joy, "Yeah," and the observers applaud. She says, "Wow, this feels good. Can this stay with me?"

SUSTAINING

My colleague and I discuss the concept of sustaining insight, gestalt learning, with the group. This group has already, in a previous session, learned about the four stages of the journey: Struggle, Paradox, Insight, Elevation. So this group is familiar with the concept of sustaining an insight in an elevation of awareness.

The client comes up and works with me and my colleague to map on the chalkboard the emotional process she feels she just went through. The symbols for **struggle paradox insight elevation** *are all used. This allows the client to gain a* **metacognitive awareness** *of her process: her ECF (executive control function) is drawn into her conscious awareness. This also gives her terminology to explain her process to the group. The group members are asked to make notes on (and map) their own journeys as they watched this client's process.*

IMAGINING AS A TOOL

I explain to clients that imagination is a process of exploring ideas, concepts, possibilities, and **developing new neural pathways in the brain, new perceptual processing. Imagination uses creativity functions of the mind and brain.** *I add that visualization is part of this creative process. (I tell clients how I was once hit with a neurological condition which required that I visualize rewiring myself with new pathways for neural messages to travel within and throughout my brain and body. I succeeded in either developing or repairing pathways that messages could travel. I had either imagined that this had happened or it actually had happened. Either way, I succeeded in helping myself.)*

VISUALIZING TO FORM NEW NEURAL PATHWAYS, NEW LEARNINGS, SUSTAINED AHAs

The clients discuss with each other the concept that the mind and brain can imagine/visualize moving the problem pattern outside the brain and body. I note that this can allow the SELF to engage its brain's ECF, to gain greater conscious awareness of the process.

I add that this has been a first process of speaking to the mind and brain, of taking some degree of conscious control of what is going on under the radar in there.

I also note that in this process, the client who had done this with her problem addiction, had placed it in one chair, and then found it within herself in the other chair. Then, she had had the addition speak to itself – speak from the open chair to itself within her in the other (seemingly also open) chair.

Simply by engaging in this imaginary or actual process, this addiction has gestalted itself, and thus revealed itself. Were there no addiction to gestalt itself, this would be a far easier process. There would be no struggle, no resistance, as there would be no addiction pattern to symbolically or actually pull out of the self.

I add that: when my colleague had taken the addiction out of the room by removing **both** *chairs, the imaginary or actual exit of the addiction(s) had been further gestalted. I note that this takes place on both the conscious level and on the sub- and perhaps even unconscious levels. All levels of the SELF feels this, is aware of this.*

And the client, well she had been left behind with her SELF.

"Can this mean I'm free now?" The client asks me and the group.

I respond, **"What do you think, how do you want to explain this to yourself? After all, this is happening in your own mind, so the way you process this is up to you."**

"I want this sort of thing to work for me. I am committing to continue working this way, gaining more and more conscious control of what is going on inside my mind."

ALLOWING THE
SLOWEST, MOST PROLONGED, ONGOING AHA
FOR THE MOST LASTING CHANGE

I explain, "To make this work, doing this exercise again and again until it becomes part of your neural memory is a good idea. Ideally, the first many times, you do this with guidance, with a trained psychotherapist or guide to be present for you as you do this."

At this point, several other group members want to arrange their chairs and take part in the process of having their addictions gestalt themselves. Again, these processes are engaging, and many who at first choose to just observe then gain interest and confidence and want to engage in the Gestalting Addiction Process for themselves.

If you ask me, these addictions want to do this as well. They actually may seek to gestalt themselves. This is likely imaginary or actual from the perspective of the brain cells and synapses participating in the gestalt. Or is it? This is up to us, the portion of ourselves who are free to force via paradox our addictions to gestalt themselves. What a paradox even this paradoxical gestalt can be.

SEEING THE PRESENCE OF MULTIPLE PARADOXES

Indeed, there is distinct synergistic power in the multiple paradoxes present and at play in the above *Addiction Gestalting Itself Process*, the obvious juxtapositioning of:

- the "empty" chair and the client in the other chair.
- the "empty chair" not being empty.
- the addiction resisting being identified, differentiated, separated, versus its strong voice.
- the addiction and the SELF.
- the addiction as part of the SELF versus it not being such.
- the client's role in the process of facilitating addiction's gestalting of itself.
- the addiction speaking to itself.
- and more.

These are just some of the multiple levels of the *paradoxical juxtapositioning of factors* **that can be guided** *to catalyze, to gestalt,* **areas of the executive control function into aware conscious level,** *to catalyze release from the insidious double bind of the invasive problem addiction pattern program.*

282

26
Navigating the
Emotional Terrain
In Gestalting Addiction

All shared in these chapters is just a start, just a brief look at the complex *Gestalting Addiction Process* that has taken me (and many of my clients) on such a profound journey into the land of the mind, heart, and soul.

Nothing about the brief examples of these *Gestalting Addiction Processes* included in the previous chapters (*Chapters 21, 24,* and *25,* for example) are meant to minimize, fictionalize, or take lightly these processes such as putting addiction in a chair and speaking to it.

Rather, the *creative imagination* is engaged as a tool in the work of consciously developing insight and learning, consciously engaging with the brain's ECF (executive control function), and of consciously directing some emotional, cognitive, and behavioral change.

Here is where the *mind/brain can gain conscious involvement in generating new options for itself.* These new options may take practice, require repeated experiences designed to train and retrain us, our brains, to develop new responses, and to engage our brains' executive control functions in their command control efforts to take us back, to unravel us, from invasive problem addiction programming.

WALK WITH OUR CLIENTS

I suggest that we psychotherapists can "walk" with our clients, guide our clients, as they move deeper into themselves, to a place where they can face, even confront, the problem addiction patterns that are inhabiting them. In *gestalting addiction:*

Places within the subconscious where the roots of one's identity live can be called into the aware conscious realm. A conscious realignment of identity of SELF can be undertaken. This is not a brief or simply overnight process. This is the matter of identifying and then unraveling from an unwanted presence, a program also weaving its way deep into the subconscious realm, even into the identity.

In the words of a client engaged in these *Gestalting the Addiction Matrix Processes (GAMPs)*, "Now that I get it, I see what is going on. Now I can tell the invasive addiction pattern program that it can no longer inhabit me." (Refer to *Chapter 13* regarding addiction *inhabiting* us.)

This facing, confronting addiction, is not only conceivable, this is something that can be done in the therapeutic **Gestalting the Addiction Matrix Process Steps** (GAMPS) I have developed to apply in these *Gestalting Addiction Processes:*

GAMP STEP ONE: We are now activating the metacognition, the thinking about thinking role of our mind's executive control function (ECF). Here is where we can turn a *conscious eye* on the workings of the invasive problem addiction programming.

GAMP STEP TWO: Coming face to face with the problem addiction pattern program is both paradoxical and pivotal in itself. Simply being able to go to such an (imaginary or actual) locus in time and space, is already a major step. Here is the place in the SELF where the rubber meets the road, where the SELF confronts the addiction that has invaded it, is now masquerading as part of the SELF itself.

GAMP STEP THREE: Once coming face to face with the problem addiction pattern program, see it as separate from the self. This may be easy to do for some clients, and for others, this step may require a metaphorical, imagined, or actual unraveling of SELF from the clutches of the addiction pattern.

GAMP STEP FOUR: And then the next step calls us. Once we (our clients, ourselves) are differentiated, separated from the problem addiction pattern program (separated metaphorically or actually or both, you decide), we can not only (imagine we are or actually) speak to this problem pattern program, we can also (imagine we are or actually) hear this problem pattern program respond to us. Even imagination versus actuality presents paradox for ourselves. Let this level and energy of paradox reverberate throughout the SELF, feel what this means. Come to know the energy of paradox.

GAMP STEP FIVE: Now the highly aware clinician can see, sense, feel, the moment when the client comes face to face with the problem addiction pattern that has moved into the programming, the neural wiring of this client. This is also a coming face to face with paradox. Here is where the psychotherapist's modeling and guidance can allow this client to meet the invader, the addiction program, come face to face with the problem addiction, and "see" (sense, feel, know, generate) the conceptual, virtual space between the addiction and the SELF. Here is where conceiving of, working on developing, a boundary between the SELF and the problem addiction program intertwining with the SELF is a valuable visualization type of exercise. This boundary between SELF and addiction program draws a line right through the paradox of muddled identity.

GAMP STEP SIX: Now these understandings make more and more sense to us:

1. The dialog toward the long and lasting learning of the sustained AHA begins. Help clients understand that for AHA insights to be sustained, to truly result in lasting elevations of awareness, learning, understanding, and even behavior, momentary insights must themselves be repeated, practiced, sustained. This slow and repeated AHA leads to sustained elevation.
2. We can recognize more and more about our problem patterns. We can tag these patterns with characteristics as they move through our minds/brains, the way we tag animals in the wild to track them.
3. We can speak to our problem patterns and hear these patterns speak to us.
4. In so doing, we can further differentiate ourselves from problem addiction patterns.
5. Already, just by initiating this understanding, this problem pattern is gestalting itself. Just by being present for this, it is acknowledging its presence.
6. Anything this problem addiction pattern does or does not do in this process is the problem pattern gestalting itself:
   - If this problem pattern does not respond when we address it, it reveals its programming to remain hidden, under our conscious radar. Yet we have already identified it and put it at least conceptually outside of ourselves to confront it.
   - If this problem pattern does respond (whether this response is imaginary or actual), anything it responds with is also a gestalt of itself.

> **Basically, we have double binded our own problem addiction pattern, gestalted the trojan horse out from the under the radar of invisibility it rode into us on!!!**
> *(See figure on next page.)*

7. Like figures in an Escher print, the voice of the problem pattern program now comes out of the ground, out of the woodwork, reveals itself, already **gestalting itself** in its self-revealing. This gestalt is a form completion of itself, as seeing the "whole" picture reveals the invader, the problem addiction program.

8. Where this problem pattern had delved very deeply into our own identity, now this *Gestalting Addiction Process* is revealing the presence, the identity, of the problem addiction pattern itself—and confirming that the SELF is NOT THIS PROBLEM ADDICTION PROGRAM.

THE ART OF
ORCHESTRATING
THE TRANSFORMATIONAL JUXTAPOSITION

The highly aware psychotherapist/clinician/guide can generate and then see, sense, feel, the moment when the client comes face to face with the problem addiction program that has moved into the programming, the neural wiring of the client. Here is where guidance can allow this client to meet the addiction program, and then to come face to face with the conceptual, virtual space—boundary—between the addiction and the SELF. Again, conceiving of a space and then a boundary between the SELF and the problem addiction afflicting the SELF is key in this process.

TRUE PROBLEM/CHALLENGE:
TAKE YOURSELF BACK FROM THIS
INVASIVE PROBLEM PATTERN ADDICTION

THE PROBLEM PATTERN'S GOAL IS TO MERGE WITH THE HOST, WITH THE PERSON, TO FULLY INSTATE ITSELF AS THE DOMINANT PATTERN WITHIN ITS HOST.
The trigger-urge-craving addicted response cycle (pattern) below is NOT the host's pattern, it is the invasive problem addiction's pattern/program.

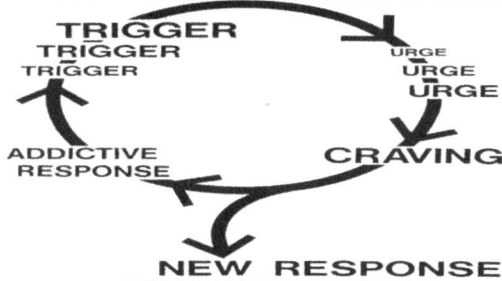

TRIGGER
TRIGGER
TRIGGER

URGE
URGE
URGE

CRAVING

ADDICTIVE RESPONSE

NEW RESPONSE

THE TRUTH ABOUT
THIS ADDICTION

THE SELF MUST FULLY KNOW AND LIVE THE TRUTH WHICH IS:
I, THE HOST, AM NOT THIS INVASIVE PROBLEM ADDICTION PATTERN/PROGRAM.
I MUST DO EVERYTHING I CAN, NOW THAT I KNOW THIS, TO TAKE MYSELF BACK FROM THIS INVADER.

Here is the **JUXTAPOSITION PRESSURE** we have now placed on this invader, this problem addiction pattern programming: NOW ADDICTION, I SEE YOU, you are called out now, *you are caught in your own paradoxical double bind*, the one you have been programming me to stay trapped in, to not see the existence of.
I AM NOT YOU. I WILL HOLD YOU BACK,
STOP YOU NOW.

NO LONGER BE OBLIVIOUS

Virtually oblivious to the double bind itself, many clinicians and practitioners proceed in their work. Indeed, much of the excellent and well meaning addiction therapy and addiction treatment seeks to promote healthy changes in behavior, and does so without addressing in depth the matters discussed in this book, *GESTALTING ADDICTION*. And certainly, the linking of the emotional with the cognitive processes is being done very well in a range of treatment and therapy contexts.[83]

I do want to note here, even to highlight and emphasize here, that it is time we do address the gestalting of deeply embedded addictions, the catalytic nature of actually *gestalting addiction*, that I offer in this book. It is time to utilize this *gestalting addiction* and realize its maximum positive potential. It is time that authentic and highly informed professional training in this realm, such as the *Gestalting Addiction Processes* I have introduced herein, be made available.

I have shared much of my journey in this book, for me a journey of the intellect, the heart, and the soul. My goal with *GESTALTING ADDICTION* is to further open minds and hearts and souls to new views, new possibilities, new understandings of what we are doing. This is just an introduction to my thinking. I will share more upon contact....

With sincere gratitude to my dear clients whose processes, recoveries, and openings to new levels of themselves, their own hearts, minds, and souls, inspires me and brings tears to my eyes almost every day. Dr. Angela Brownemiller

---

[83] Examples include CBT, Cognitive Behavioral Therapy, and DBT, Dialectical Behavioral Therapy, and their original version, Rational Emotive Therapy.

Epilog:
The Truth
About Us

If we listen, we can hear. We humans are calling ourselves to see what is happening to us, within us, around us. We are speaking to ourselves from deep inside ourselves, telling ourselves to pay attention to the messages we are sending ourselves. If we listen we can hear ourselves calling us to be as clear and honest with ourselves about ourselves, about who and what we are, as we can be -- *and* to be as clear and honest with ourselves about those around us, about who and what these persons are, as we can be.

This is not an easy calling. The answers are not readily found and applied. In fact, just when we think we see the whole picture, or something close to the whole picture, we do not. There is always more to know, there are always more dots to connect, there is always another segment of the whole, of the form of the SELF -- to find, to discover, to call forth, to gestalt.

The circle of our search is always infinite. The closer we get to answers, to completing the search, the closer we are to knowing we will always have more to discover.

Just as we think we are finally completing the puzzle of self, we see there are more pieces still to be discovered, that there is not yet a completion of the whole picture. No matter how close we are to completing the picture, solving the riddle of ourselves, there is always more to see and know, there are always more dots to connect.

This infinite search for the truth about ourselves reveals itself in so many ways. We find we are creatures living with incomplete knowledge about ourselves, even while telling ourselves (or our brains telling us) we know so much, or even know it all, see the whole (or enough of the whole) picture. In essence, we are trapped in a never complete picture of ourselves, our realities, our behaviors. And we become hooked on this incomplete picture, dependent upon it for sustenance. (At least we believe in our existence enough to at least believe we exist.)

In this sense, human beings tend to choose to tell themselves that: they know what is going on, they see the whole picture, therefore their conclusions about their reality are accurate. Nevertheless, anything our brains tell us we know is a merely a construction of a picture based on pieces of the whole reality.

Yes, we humans tend to believe what our brains are wired to tell us to believe, to take what data we have and paste it together to form a picture of reality.

We do this for the sake of living within that picture. All human beings are carrying around brains that are wired to support their belief in whatever incomplete picture they ascribe to, to tell themselves they live within a complete picture when they know, they truly know, there is no completing. The circle of self never closes, is always evolving, discovering. It is this infinite DISCOVERY that is our journey. (See the book, KEYS TO PERSONAL DISCOVERY, where I further detail this matter.)

We humans are wired to become addicted to ways of being, seeing, living, behaving. In this sense, we are all addicted to our realities or to what we have come to believe are our realities. Much of this addiction has great survival value. And much of this addiction does not have survival value, may actually be quite counter survival. Differentiating between healthy addictions and their patterns and unhealthy (problem) addictions and their patterns is essential and must be continuous.

So here we are, beings who know what we think we know, based on our completion of an incomplete picture, based on our brain's reading of incomplete data to tell us we know what we think we know. And our brains, they are working so hard to captain this ship, the ship of US, to hold us whole in the face of so many invasions of our boundaries, of our identities, of our SELVES.

Let's join together in this understanding of all that our species is facing, the challenges to our survival both:
- in external biospheric and political environments, and
- in our internal spiritual and biological, even synaptic, environments where the struggle for our survival is equally momentous.

Praying for the future of humanity,
and for those souls
who have not survived this Earthly passage,
and for everyone else who is here.
Every moment matters,

Dr. Angela®

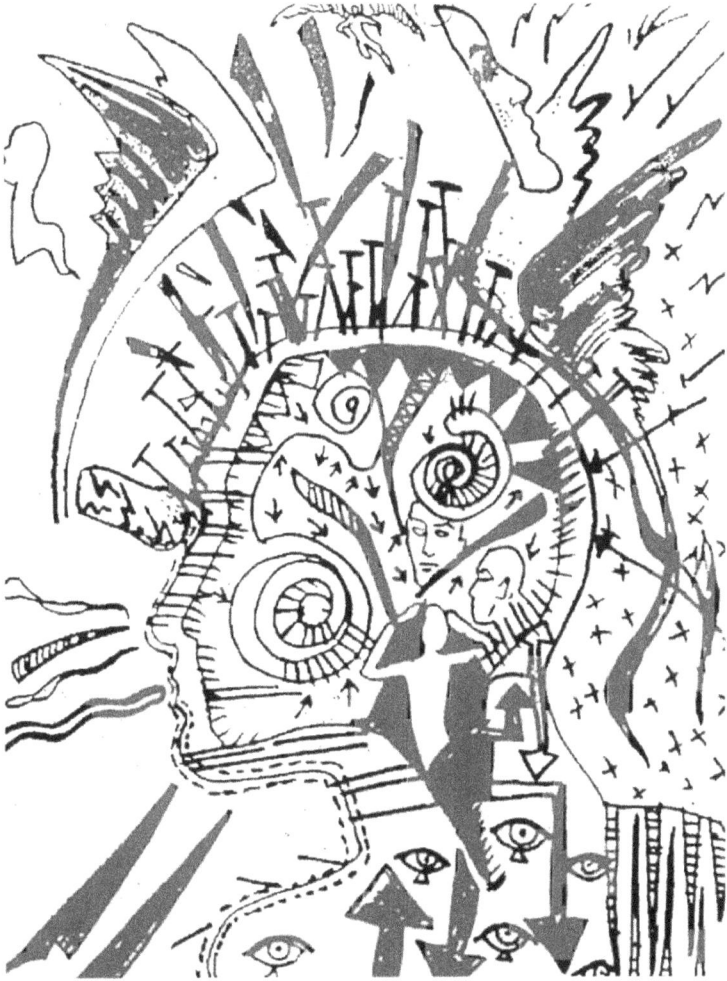

printed with permission, anonymous art therapy workshop participant

In the Circle of Self

BOOKLIST AND RECOMMENDED READING

Some of the books by Dr. Angela Brownemiller include:

****

Seeing Beyond Our Line of Sight:
Consciously Moving Through Life's Changes, Transitions, and Deaths

****

The Going Conscious Process:
Steps and Practices for Heightening Conscious
Awareness, Shifts, Transmigrations of Focus, LEAPs of Self

****

Overriding the Extinction Scenario, Part II:
Raising the Bar on the Evolution of the Human Species

****

Overriding the Extinction Scenario, Part I:
Detecting the Bar on the Evolution of the Human Species

****

How to Die and Survive, Books One, Two and Three:
Concepts for Living and Dying

****

Unveiling the Hidden Instinct:
Understanding Our
Interdimensional Survival Awareness

****

Keys to Self: Your Next Steps to YOU

****

Adventures in Changes, Transitions, and Deaths:
Primer for Life's Minor and Major Challenges and Passages

****

Transcending Addiction and Other Afflictions

****

For Knowing No Hurt No Harm:
Hidden, Subtle, and Obvious Aspects of
Intimate and Other Partner
Abuse, Violence, and Terror

****

GestaltING Addiction:
Speaking Truth to Addiction –
Its Power, Definition, Theory, Therapy, and Treatment

****

Seeing the Hidden Face of Addiction:
Detecting and Confronting this Invasive Presence

See also...

International Collection on Addictions (four volumes)
Editor, Angela Browne-Miller (Browne-Miller)
Volume One: Faces of Addiction Then And Now
Volume Two: Psychobiological Profiles
Volume Three: Characteristics and Treatment Perspectives
Volume Four: Behavioral Addictions from Concept to Compulsion

Violence and Abuse in Society (four volumes)
Editor, Angela Browne-Miller (Browne-miller)
Volume One: Fundamentals, Effects, and Extremes
Volume Two: Setting, Age, Gender, and Other Key Elements
Volume Three: Psychological, Ritual, Sexual, and Trafficking Issues
Volume Four: Faces of Intimate Partner Violence

Note:
The books listed on this and the previous page
have been listed on Amazon.com.
If not finding these books on Amazon.com,
contact local or online bookstores, and or Amazon.com,
and or DrAngela@DrAngela.com for the author's staff
and or the author, Dr. Angela Brownemiller.
Note again, this author's last name also appears as Browne-Miller.

ABOUT THE AUTHOR
Dr. Angela Brownemiller
Dr. Angela®

Dr. Angela Brownemiller, also known as Dr. Angela® (and Angela Browne-Miller), is an author, journalist, social thinker, clinician, psychotherapist, speaker, host of the Dr. Angela Hour® and Ask Dr. Angela Programs®, and founder of the Keys to Self® Programs. The views of Dr. Angela® Brownemiller are centered on the great potential of the Human mind, heart, spirit, and soul, and on the rights of all of us, who and whatever we are (or think we are). Dr. Angela Brownemiller views the Human consciousness as a wealth of opportunity for exploration, Insight, knowledge--and survival. For more information on her work, see DrAngela.com.

The works of Dr. Angela Brownemiller
(some of which are listed on the previous pages)
are brought to you by:
METATERRA® PUBLICATIONS
and other publishers.

To take part in our
online and on-ground events, workshops, and trainings
contact us at:
DrAngela@DrAngela.com
For personal consultations
in person, or by telephone, or online,
contact us at
DrAngela@DrAngela.com

www.DrAngela.com

Dr. Angela

What Is Unspoken

AHA!

Dr. Angela®

www.ingramcontent.com/pod-product-compliance
Lightning Source LLC
Chambersburg PA
CBHW070717280326
41926CB00087B/2400